# MAKE IT BETTER

# MAKE IT BETTER

DR ILYA KOVAR

CHANCELLOR
PRESS

# CONTENTS

## PART ONE
## ILLS AND AILMENTS
## A-Z

*page 13*

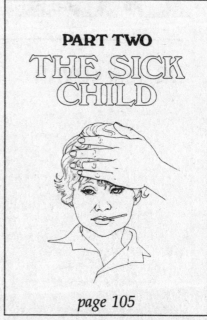

## PART TWO
## THE SICK CHILD

*page 105*

Beginning with a pictorial guide, part one contains an alphabetical listing of childhood disorders. Details include a description of the illness, how it is treated and how long it lasts.

Part two concerns looking after a sick child at home or in hospital, with advice on treating temperatures, giving medicine, relieving pain, what is the right food and when quarantine is necessary.

## PART THREE
# PREVENTION

### page 133

The routine assessment of your child's
health, visits to the dentist,
immunization, nutrition, clothing,
safety precautions, hygiene and the
avoidance of common problems are all
dealt with in part three.

## PART FOUR
# FIRST AID

### page 173

The details in part four cover a basic first
aid kit, a step-by-step guide to mouth-
to-mouth resuscitation and cardiac
massage, as well as what first aid to give
in the case of common problems.

First published in Great Britain in 1982 by
Octopus Books Limited

This 1993 edition published by Chancellor Press an imprint of
Reed Consumer Books Limited
Michelin House, 81 Fulham Road, London SW3 6RB
and Auckland, Melbourne, Singapore and Toronto

Copyright © 1993 by Reed International Books Limited

ISBN 1 8515 2475 4

A CIP catalogue record for this book is available at the British Library

Printed and bound in the United Kingdom by The Bath Press, Avon

Illustrations by Coral Mula

*Dedicated to*
*Cynthia, Simon,*
*Benjamin and Sarah*

# INTRODUCTION

Looking after children is fun for a doctor; it is an opportunity to deal with a future rather than a past as children grow, change and develop. For a parent a child represents posterity.

There are many books offering advice on child care but no book is a substitute for practice and experience. This book is not intended to provide all the answers, or to be a diagnostic aid or treatment manual, but is rather an attempt to offer background information and a ready reference to common childhood problems. You will find that one of the commonest concepts in the book is 'When in doubt call your doctor . . .', you should, however, trust your own instinct and commonsense, as this is often the best guide when considering questions about your child's health. It is always best to be safe and seek advice early or even unnecessarily; children can get ill (and better!) very quickly and the margin of safety can be quite small, while the margin for error is wide. The child health care system overall works well and, used wisely, can help the individual parent ensure the physical and emotional interests of their developing child.

Children, and their problems, differ at the varying ages and stages of development. You may find some ages better than others. The baby who is delightful and helpless turns into the

crawling and walking menace of a one year old,
the tearaway toddler (tiring but lots of fun), the
irritating, demanding and frustrating
preschooler (but ever so interesting), the
worrying (to some) school age child and the
even more worrying (to others) adolescent. Each
stage has its pleasures and drawbacks. Most
parents stop worrying when they are
grandparents! Children for many parents are
nothing but pleasure, for others only
aggravation while for the rest of us the truth lies
somewhere in the middle. Child rearing is an
intuitive art, you need only commonsense, a
little judgement, and possibly a little luck, to get
it right. No two children are the same so there
can be no universal rules; growing up involves
drama, and mistakes by both parent and child,
but they do it in the end. The parents' task
(some would say, obligation) is to provide
understanding and physical and emotional
security. There should be no unreasonable
expectations of the child (not every boy will play
rugby) and then there will be no later feeling of
disappointment, failure or inner conflict in
either the parent or child. Ideally the
relationship should be one of mutual respect;
the child is not an extension of the parent but
rather must be allowed to be an individual in his
own right. Some develop sooner than others,
are good at one thing and not another, some
succeed and some fail. Unnecessary pressure on
a child who is 'not ready' for the next
developmental stage whether educational,

physical or emotional, breeds only unhappiness and resentment. The problem is usually the parents' and not the child's.

Normal is a relative term when referring to children and you must understand it in relation to your child. A change from 'normal' behaviour might suggest illness or worry; what is normal for one child in the family might not be for another. It can be normal for a child with a particular illness to behave in one way, while for another child without this problem the implications of the behaviour pattern may be different. It is normal for a one year old to cry because of separation anxiety, when his mother leaves the room; a three year old should be more independent. You should also recognise as normal certain emotional reactions you may have; babies are not always fun, children can get you down and with tiredness you might be badtempered, you may even actively seek ways of palming them off, while the same piece of behaviour may on one occasion not bother you but at another time make you angry. These emotions are normal and do not represent rejection, all parents feel them at some stage. There are always periods of calm and periods of storm, children must learn to cope with you (and life) as you must with them. Recognise, too, that your 'hang-ups' may play a role in your response to particular behaviour; sex play by children may threaten you but to the child it is innocent, enjoyable, not harmful to development and in fact normal. He will not

have prejudices but may pick up yours.
Although exposed to many outside pressures
and influences, the main determinant of the
child's long-term thinking and attitudes is
usually within the home.

Children with a problem, a protracted illness
or a physical handicap need special
consideration. They, too, are normal in their
own way. Expectations must be geared to the
possible; with care, affection and
encouragement they can lead happy and
meaningful lives. The birth of a damaged child is
a traumatic experience. The parents may reject
the baby and should be regarded with
understanding and not be condemned. They
need to grieve the loss of normality as they
perceived it, the loss of a dream and the loss of
their own aspirations for their child. When the
grieving is over, they learn that the child is not
imperfect but rather is normal and perfect in his
own way, somebody to be cherished, loved and
entitled to his own future and happiness.
Understanding needs to be offered to both
parent and child, there is no place for pity or
contempt.

Immigrant families, too, have special needs
and problems linked to their different customs,
language and expectations. The children, keen
to be accepted by peers, may rebel against the
old ways. An understanding of the conflicts and
needs of the families is necessary; the system,
too, lets them down.

Child health begins before conception; a

healthy mother backed by good nutrition, good family support, good antenatal care and a safe delivery will give each new baby the best chance of a good future. After birth, good nutrition, commonsense by parents, intelligent use of the health service and a safe society are the best safeguards of that future. Illness is unfortunately, however, an everpresent evil; there are very few truly nasty illnesses in childhood, most come and go, some quickly some slowly. Children often grow out of many of the common ailments and medical interference is not always necessary. Time is on-side in the young years. The effect of a particular problem also may change with age and allowance for this may need to be made. Each problem is different. For most common things your judgement is the best guide and when in doubt seek advice. Your family doctor or local paediatrician is always available to help you and your child to cope with a particular problem, to provide a cure if one is available, or just to give reassurance. This book, I hope, will also help in providing information.

I hope no offence has been caused by using 'he' throughout the text; 'she' could just as easily have been used. A coin was tossed!

*Ilya Kovar*

# PART ONE
# ILLS AND AILMENTS

# A-Z

# Your guide to the A-Z

*Most illnesses in children do not distinguish between boys and girls; in this index one applies equally to the other. It should be remembered that there are common and uncommon conditions; do not assume that because your child has a problem in a particular*

*part of the body the cause will be listed under that part alone. Those conditions, such as emotional and behavioural problems, which do not obviously apply to a fixed part of the body are not listed here but can be found in the A to Z. For ease of reference, both medical and common names are listed here.*

### Hair/Scalp
| | |
|---|---|
| Abnormal hair loss | 54 |
| Alopecia | 54 |
| Baby dandruff | 38 |
| Cradle cap | 38 |
| Excess hair growth | 54 |
| Head lice | 55 |
| Nits | 55 |
| Pediculus capitis | 55 |
| Scalp seborrhoea | 82 |
| Scurf | 84 |
| Seborrhoeic dermatitis | 38 |

### Trunk
| | |
|---|---|
| Abnormal curvature of the spine | 89 |
| Asthma | 20 |
| Bee stings | 90 |
| Bronchiolitis | 28 |
| Bronchitis | 29 |
| Bruising | 89 |
| Cavernous naevus | 68 |
| Chicken pox | 30 |
| Cystic fibrosis | 41 |
| German measles | 51 |
| Glandular fever | 51 |
| Heart murmur | 56 |
| Hypertrichosis | 54 |
| Impetigo | 60 |
| Infectious Mononucleosis | 51 |
| Measles | 65 |
| Moles | 69 |
| Obesity | 72 |
| Pertussis | 101 |
| Pneumonia | 76 |
| Respiratory tract problems | 79 |
| Ringworm | 80 |
| Roseola infantum | 80 |
| Rubella | 51 |
| Scarlet fever | 82 |
| Scoliosis | 89 |
| Spontaneous bruising | 89 |
| Varicella | 30 |
| Wheezy bronchitis | 101 |
| Whooping cough | 101 |

### Eyes
| | |
|---|---|
| 99 | Astigmatism |
| 99 | Colour blindness |
| 33 | Conjunctivitis |
| 89 | Cross eyes |
| 98 | Hyperopia |
| 89 | Lazy eye |
| 98 | Long sightedness |
| 98 | Myopia |
| 92 | Periorbital oedema |
| 98 | Short sightedness |
| 89 | Squint |
| 33 | Sticky eye |
| 89 | Strabismus |
| 91 | Stye |
| 92 | Swelling around the eyes |
| 98 | Vision defects |

### Ears
| | |
|---|---|
| 44 | Ear ache |
| 52 | Glue ears |
| 64 | Mastoiditis |
| 66 | Middle ear infection |
| 73 | Otitis externa |
| 66 | Otitis media |
| 73 | Outer ear infection |
| 52 | Secretory otitis media |
| 100 | Wax |

### Neck and Throat
| | |
|---|---|
| 38 | Cough |
| 39 | Croup |
| 39 | Laryngitis |
| 94 | Pharyngitis |
| 94 | Sore throat |
| 94 | Tonsillitis |
| 103 | Torticollis |
| 103 | Wry neck |

### Hips
| | |
|---|---|
| 75 | Perthes' diseases |

### Legs
| | |
|---|---|
| 28 | Bow legs |
| 63 | Knock-knees |
| 73 | Osteomyelitis |
| 79 | Rickets |

## Abdominal Pain (Tummy pain)

The causes of abdominal pain affecting children differ from those affecting adults, for example, peptic ulcers and gall bladder troubles which are common in adults are rare in children. The site and type of abdominal pain in a child do not give all that much of a clue as to its source; pain from the urinary tract and pain from the gut can feel precisely the same and occur in the same place. Therefore, blood tests, urine tests and X-rays are often needed to distinguish between them.

Pain due to causes which may require surgical treatment, for example, appendicitis, is usually accompanied by vomiting. If you feel the abdomen, it is tender and tense to the touch and the child may wince and cry out. With psychological pain, in the so-called bellyacher, the tummy is usually soft and no abnormalities are found, despite repeated complaints of pain. The pain is often associated with certain identifiable events, such as school, may be cyclic and rarely occurs at times when the child is doing things he enjoys. Tests, including X-rays, are often necessary to exclude a physical cause which needs treatment. The pain, when diagnosed, should not be disregarded and the child needs to be treated with some understanding; it is always easy to label a pain as psychological and then when the real thing comes along to ignore it and make a terrible mistake.

Take care not to give analgesics, such as paracetamol or aspirin, which will mask the pain and thereby possibly delay the diagnosis of something serious. If there are associated features, such as temperature, pain on passing urine and so on, then advice should be sought. Most pains are due to simple causes, such as constipation or a viral illness causing the abdominal glands to swell, and require only simple remedies (such as local heat). Some pains, however, can be due to serious causes, which require active treatment, such as surgery. The parent must exercise judgement as to when and how worried to be. A tender-to-touch abdomen is often a good guide to seriousness; if your child will not let you touch his tummy you should see your doctor.

## Abnormal Curvature of the Spine *(See Spine, Abnormal Curvature of on page 89)*

## Abnormal Hair Loss *(See Hair Loss, Abnormal on page 54)*

## Abscess

An abscess can occur in any part of the body. It is a walled-off, localized area of infection. There may be a fever, the child is unwell and there are symptoms related to the site of the abscess. If it is in the lung, for example, the child may have a cough and difficulty in breathing. If it is in the skin there would be a visibly red, inflamed, painful and raised area. A boil by comparison is smaller but in some ways can be considered as a small abscess. Antibiotics are often prescribed but some form of surgical drainage is often required. Occasionally the abscess comes to a head and bursts spontaneously releasing the pus that is inside it, thereby curing itself. If the abscess is inside the body and bursts, there will be spreading infection and the child will be really quite ill, requiring hospital care.

## Acne *(Acne Vulgaris)*

Acne is caused by an infection and inflammation of the oil-producing sebaceous glands of the skin; the gland (or follicle) becomes plugged with infected skin oil. Acne can affect the face, shoulders, back and scalp. It is a virtually universal complaint of adolescence and can be regarded as physiological: it affects appearance and not health. It is not in itself infectious and is not passed from one person to another by contact. Acne occurs in cycles and usually ends after puberty is complete. Boys are more commonly affected than girls. The cause is not known but is probably related to changes in the skin oil (sebum) production at the time of puberty together with a superimposed bacterial infection. The spots or lesions are known as comedones. These may be open lesions (known as blackheads), where the plug of the impacted follicle is seen, or closed (whiteheads), when only a pinpoint opening of the follicle is obvious. Scratching the spots may introduce and spread infection causing the acne to become worse; occasionally whole areas become inflamed and scars are more likely to form.

Many forms of commercial preparation are advertised to treat acne; some work, most do not. Greasy cosmetics and hair preparations should be avoided. The secret is careful skin and hair cleansing to remove surface skin fats and make the skin less oily. You should be aware, however, that if you do it too often in any one day it may be harmful and the skin will be irritated. Agents which have a drying and peeling quality, such as sulphur compounds or salicylic acid, should be used. They should be applied after the skin has been thoroughly washed with a medicated soap. Do not squeeze the spots. This will break the follicles and whereas it might clear an individual comedone, there is a risk of introducing infection. Diet probably plays no role in the cause, but many teenagers feel that an individual food, for example chocolate, may be involved. Preparations containing a vitamin A derivative seem to work in clearing acne but do take several weeks to have an obvious effect. Doctors often prescribe a course of antibiotics to clear the skin of secondary infection and then recommend a period of careful skin cleansing, mainly using soap. In severe cases a short course of oral steroid drugs might even be considered. Ultra-violet light (natural ultra-violet light comes from the sun) may also occasionally help by drying the skin. Natural sunshine is best; ultra-violet lamps can be used provided you are careful. They should only be used for short periods of time and the eyes should be carefully shielded, since superficial burns are a real risk. The best treatment is usually time!

Infantile acne affects some infants. Scarring is rare and usually no treatment is necessary; it improves spontaneously by two to three months.

# Allergic Rhinitis *(See Hay Fever on page 55)*

**Alopecia** *(See Hair Loss, Abnormal on page 54)*

## Anaemia

Anaemia is a condition resulting from a decreased number of circulating red blood cells or a deficiency in the oxygen carrying chemical (haemoglobin) in those cells. The child will be lethargic and look pale. He may be breathless with mild exertion or even at rest; a small baby who is anaemic may have difficulty feeding and be puffing and panting while taking milk.

There are many causes of anaemia: the red cells may not be produced in sufficient quantities; they may be abnormally broken down or it may be that blood is being lost in some way. Some of the causes are minor, while others can be more serious. The important things are to be aware that anaemia might exist and, if it is discovered, to look for the specific cause, as treatment will depend on this. The diagnosis is made by a blood test. In childhood the most common reason is a simple nutritional iron deficiency. At about six months of age, if solid feeding has not been introduced, the child begins to run out of the iron he received from his mother late in pregnancy and he may become anaemic. Some doctors recommend that all babies, especially if premature, are given drops containing iron; not all doctors agree with this approach – provided there is a balanced diet by around six months, there is probably no need.

## Animal Bites

These usually happen because a family pet has become excited due to excessive teasing; occasionally the bite is due to a direct attack. Bites by farm animals sometimes occur and the treatment is just the same. The wound needs to be washed to remove saliva and any dirt or debris; running water is often adequate, and a light antiseptic then used, as secondary infection of the wound can occur. In some cases the wound may be deep enough to require stitches. An anti-tetanus injection is always advisable after an animal bite. The risk of rabies, although quite rare and unlikely, should always be borne in mind. Your doctor will advise you.

It is rarely necessary to get rid of a family animal. The problem is often due to the child's behaviour and only occasionally does an animal become 'violent'.

## Appendicitis

The appendix, as an organ, serves no useful function; it is an evolutionary remnant. If the appendix becomes blocked with bacteria, inflammation sets in and there is a risk that with swelling it will burst. Appendicitis can occur at any age, even adults can be affected.

The child complains of pain which begins around the umbilicus and then moves towards the right lower quarter of the abdomen. This will generally be accompanied by a mild temperature, nausea and vomiting. The inflamed appendix may irritate nearby structures, such as the bladder, which becomes painful and causes the child to pass urine more frequently. The child looks ill and is obviously in pain, the abdomen is tender to touch. A viral inflammation of the abdominal lymph nodes can mimic appendicitis and it is often very difficult to distinguish between the two illnesses. Usually the diagnosis is made at surgery! The treatment of acute appendicitis is an operation to remove the appendix; the wait-and-see approach risks a rupture and the formation of a local abscess or a generalized inflammation of the lining of the abdominal cavity (peritonitis).

Occasionally there is only a slight inflammation. This is known as the grumbling appendix and pain may be present on and off for weeks. Antibiotics are occasionally used in this situation but surgery is the only effective treatment. The operation is relatively simple; the child is up and about in a matter of days.

## Asthma

Spasms of the bronchial breathing tubes, from whatever cause, will lead to a wheeze being heard as the child breathes. The wheeze is caused by air turbulence which is created by the narrowing of the tubes. The child may need to struggle to get air both in and out past the obstruction. If the obstruction is severe then added oxygen may need to be given.

True asthma usually has an allergic cause, often runs in

families and can be quite severe and distressing. Asthma attacks may be seasonal (more common in spring) or when the child is exposed to whatever it is he is allergic to. The bronchial walls produce mucus and go into spasm. In severe cases (usually multiple allergies) the bronchi are constantly in a minor degree of spasm, with a feeling that the asthma is ever present.

The treatment is divided into acute treatment for the attack, regular medicines to limit the number and severity of the attacks, and prevention. The drugs used to limit and treat the attack are collectively known as bronchodilators; these work by causing the bronchial tubes to relax, limiting the spasm and hence the obstruction. The drugs can be given by mouth or are inhaled as a fine powder by being turned into a spray by a nebulizer. Hospital treatment may occasionally be necessary.

Allergy tests may be done by the doctor to find out what the child is allergic to. A common allergy is one to house dust or more particularly to a little mite (a sort of germ) which lives in dust; regular cleaning, vacuuming and damp dusting help, as does avoidance of feather pillows and bed covers. Animal fur and pollens also cause allergies in some children. Occasionally, in severe cases with proven allergy the doctor might recommend a course of desensitizing injections (to the allergy).

Emotion is often blamed as a cause of acute asthma attacks or for making asthma worse. It is difficult to say what causes what – the emotional upset the asthma or vice versa. Some attacks can, however, be related to periods of increased stress, such as exams, home problems and so on.

It is commonly asked whether an asthmatic child's activity should be restricted. In general the answer is no. He will restrict himself if necessary. The child should be treated as normal and not as though he were handicapped. The school should, however, be told what to do if he has an attack.

Asthma usually gets better with age.

**Astigmatism** *(See section (b) of Vision Defects on page 99)*

**Athlete's Foot** *(See Ringworm on page 80)*

**Baby Dandruff** *(See Cradle Cap on page 38)*

## Bed Wetting (Enuresis)

Bed wetting or enuresis in young children is a common occurrence (about ten per cent of five to six year olds wet their beds) but causes considerable anxiety both to parents and children. There are two basic types of bed wetting. Firstly, there is what is known as primary bed wetting, where the child has never been completely dry, though some weeks are better than others. The cause is usually slow development, where toilet training is incomplete, expectations are too high and the nappies are taken away too soon. Occasionally there is a medical cause, such as a urinary tract infection (see page 97) or a structural abnormality of the urinary tract. Secondary bed wetting is usually a behavioural problem; the child is normally dry but then starts to wet the bed again at night. Usually this occurs when the child is around four to seven years old, as a result of some upset either at home or at school; often a new baby on the scene is the cause.

If either type of bed wetting persists, see your doctor. He will then examine your child to exclude all known medical problems which lead to frequency or loss of control. If there is, in fact, a medical cause, then treatment of it may solve the bed wetting problem, too. Once the doctor is satisfied he is dealing with ordinary bed wetting, then he may recommend several approaches to the parent.

Firstly, you should not give the child a drink last thing at night and you should encourage him to empty his bladder before going to bed. Secondly, a star chart is useful as it allows the child to monitor his own progress. (Stars are marked on the chart for each dry night.) When he has a particularly good week, he should be praised and possibly be positively rewarded with some sort of special treat. This praise should be withheld during a bad week but there must be no blame or punishment. Occasionally special pads with alarms are used. The bell rings when the pad is first wet, this wakes the child in time for him to use the toilet. The alarm method is not always effective. Drug treatment may be justified in persistent cases; the drug lightens sleep, so that the child may be more aware of a full bladder.

The child who is wet regularly during the day (not the occasional accident, that is) is of more concern, as this usually represents a psychological cry for help. Your doctor needs to be consulted and careful probing as to the possible cause should be carried out.

## Bee Stings *(See Stings on page 90)*

## Behaviour Disorders

These are of major concern to the average parent and include such common problems as lying, shyness, stealing, compulsive behaviour, temper tantrums, cheating and destructive behaviour. All are to some extent normal or variants of normal, particularly in the younger age groups. It is only when the behaviour pattern is persistent and excessive that it goes beyond the bounds of acceptable normality and help should be sought. Consult your doctor or paediatrician; if he is concerned, he may seek extra advice from a child psychologist or psychiatrist. If the cause can be identified and treated, the problem is usually resolved. Occasionally all that is needed is time.

### (a) *Stealing*
The young preschool child often is not able to distinguish between what belongs to him and what belongs to others. Toys are frequently borrowed without permission, but this is not stealing. The child of school age is usually old enough to know better and here stealing is a social problem. It may only take place at home or at school, for example the child may regularly

steal money or some item from his mother's purse. In this case it usually indicates an underlying emotional problem – the child is trying to tell his mother something! Occasionally stealing is due to insecurity or to greed, the child feels left out because his peers have certain possessions which he does not have.

Stealing may also be due to habit and bad example. The child has learnt from either parents or older brothers and sisters. A child who regularly steals is in need of professional help from a child psychologist. Punishment is not the treatment, the underlying reason (e.g. home difficulties) needs to be investigated and resolved.

## (b) *Lying*

The telling of lies is worrying when a child is old enough to know the difference between true deception and exaggeration. The preschool child often tells tall tales based on fantasy and exaggeration. These stories are told for effect, the aim is not to deceive. Occasionally a lie is told to avoid displeasure, particularly from the parent, such as when a favourite object has been broken and an explanation needs to be made. This is not uncommon and is normal.

The lie that is told for positive gain, however, is of more concern. Here the child does know the difference between right and wrong. The need for and importance of truth, however, have not been sufficiently emphasized. An older child who continually tells lies is usually crying out for help or for love. The problem is one of general insecurity and there is often a background of domestic strife. Occasionally professional counselling from a child psychologist is required.

## (c) *Shyness*

Shyness represents social withdrawal because of insecurity or mistrust of adults or peers. It is not uncommon when a child goes to a new school after a house move or when he first meets strangers. Don't make too much fuss about his shyness or you will make it worse next time. It is rarely a persisting problem and with sympathetic handling usually settles down and the child becomes more sociable and outgoing. It occasionally helps to invite other children to play on home territory; this gives the child confidence as he feels less threatened here and therefore has more opportunity to become outgoing.

## (d) *Temper Tantrums*

Temper tantrums are extremely common in preschool children. They occur at that period of life when the child is learning to become independent but has not yet acquired all the necessary skills. Temper tantrums are an attention-seeking device, the child needs an audience, and they represent a reaction to some frustration. The child will usually shout and scream rather than cry and may fall to the floor and kick his legs about. He may bang his head.

It is important to remain calm, although this is often not easy, particularly when the tantrum occurs in a public place, causing considerable embarrassment. The child should be taken away from the situation causing the frustration. If the parent becomes agitated the child is achieving his aim. Distraction is one of the best ways of ending the scene. You must be positive and not merely suggest an alternative. For example, do not say, "Shall we go out?", say "We are going out."

When the tantrum occurs, approach it with indifference and offer a distraction. Don't fight it, don't reason and don't use force. Learning to cope with frustration is a normal part of growing up. Temper tantrums are more common when the child has no set limits on his behaviour and discipline in the home is inconsistent. Young children are often smart and manipulative, particularly if they are used to getting their own way, are over-indulged or over-protected. Alternatively, if the home is over-strict, temper tantrums represent a form of rebellion and a battle of wills.

In the older child temper tantrums can be turned on other children as a form of aggression. In these children the basis is often inconsistent discipline. They may be used to being threatened with a certain punishment which is rarely carried out, so their behaviour is not adequately held within "limits" and the aggression then may be a reaction to what they interpret as parental rejection. Alternatively, it may be a rebellion against excessive discipline at home. If the child's attempts at independence are thwarted by constant negative comments from the parents, he will be very frustrated and feel that there is no reasonable outlet for his emotions. If the tantrums become excessive help should be sought. The doctor will need to especially exclude any underlying cause which can be remedied; for example a sensory deficit, such as mild deafness which has not been recognized, can cause extreme frustration in the child which when corrected can effect a considerable behavioural change.

## (e) *Breath Holding*

Breath holding attacks are common in the first two years of life (but may occur up to five years). A child may hold his breath, become blue, even lose consciousness and have abnormal movements similar to convulsions. There is, however, no increased risk of fits later on in life. The behaviour is generally used by the child as a means of drawing attention to himself and represents a reaction to frustration; it is a form of temper tantrum. This may be due to the fact that you have said "No" to him or have taken away a favourite toy.

Breath holding attacks are slightly more common in girls than boys and are more widespread where other children have been seen to do the same thing or if the child has a deprived background. The best treatment is to ignore the behaviour if possible and try to pretend it is not happening. The child must not be allowed to feel he is accomplishing anything with this sort of behaviour or it will become recurrent. Should breath holding attacks become too frequent, it is advisable to seek advice from your doctor. Occasionally some form of sharp stimulation, such as a shake or light slap on the bottom or cheek, is needed if the child is going blue and seems to be losing consciousness. Usually he will take a gasp and start breathing again.

One should note also that occasionally breath holding is associated with severe discomfort or pain. In these attacks, however, the child is usually pale and limp rather than tense and blue. Try to find the painful area (see page 74).

## (f) *Compulsive Behaviour*

Compulsive ritual actions are common in children; they are used as delaying tactics at bedtime or in the older child they take the form of things that are done, or specifically avoided, in order to ward off, for example, bad luck. They may represent feelings of insecurity, anger or frustration, which a child can often not express in words but which he needs to draw your attention to in some way; he gains some relief and comfort by his compulsive behaviour.

Compulsive behaviour taken to extremes generally represents emotional insecurity. Head banging is such an example in younger children. Here the child repeatedly bangs his head against objects such as the mattress or the side of his cot. It usually stops spontaneously. Head banging can occur in normal children and is harmless. It also happens in children with sensory deficits, such as blindness, and in children with mental retardation, where it represents a need for repetitive and alternative stimulation. The best treatment for children with this problem is to try to distract them, as a short-term measure but also to investigate and treat the cause as a long-term solution. It should also be noted that there has been the suggestion that chronic head bangers might be at risk of developing eye cataracts; should your child be a chronic head banger then it may be worthwhile seeking the opinion of an eye doctor when he gets older.

## (g) *Cheating*
Every child at some stage in his life cheats; cheating at school is not at all uncommon. It is only a cause for concern when cheating is persistent and represents an irrational fear of either failure or of loss of love. Usually the parents or teachers are at fault: the child is probably being pushed too hard.

## (h) *The Different Child*
Parents are often concerned that their child is different from his peers. He may be more aggressive or shy or outgoing or in some other way different. Uniformity is clearly not ideal and difference is to be encouraged. Occasionally, however, behaviour such as excessive aggression outside the group's accepted norm, may cause a child to become a social outcast and create problems in itself.

Should you be concerned that your child is significantly different from other children in his social grouping or class, then occasionally it is advisable to seek advice or reassurance. This you should get from the child's teacher or the family doctor.

# Blackheads *(See Acne on page 17)*

## Blood in the Urine or Stool (Haematuria)

You should always seek your doctor's advice if you notice blood in your child's urine or in his stool. There are many conditions, of minor and major importance, which may have caused it. Blood in the stool may be due to an anal fissure, a polyp or due to colitis; blood in the urine may suggest an infection or a nephritis (an inflammation of the kidney).

## Blue Attacks *(See Cyanosis on page 41)*

## Bow Legs (Genu Varum)

Some bowing of the legs is extremely common in the first two to three years of life. In older children (four to six years) a gap of up to 5 centimetres (2 inches) between the knees when the ankles are close together is allowed. The most common cause is an inward rotation of the bones of the leg, either the thigh or more commonly the shin bone. This usually corrects itself through the natural growth of the bones, by seven to ten years of age. If there is bowing of only one leg or the bowing is severe and has not corrected itself by around seven to ten years, then an orthopaedic opinion is necessary. Rickets (see page 79) can cause bowing of the legs.

## Breath Holding *(See section (e) of Behaviour Disorders on page 26)*

## Bronchiolitis

This is a severe infection of the lower respiratory tract (see page 79) involving inflammation of the small air passages of the lungs. It generally affects the younger infant (up to about eighteen months). The illness occurs in epidemics and is due to a virus. It generally starts as a cold which goes down to the chest causing the child to have difficulty breathing, appear distressed, have indrawing of the chest, a wheeze and occasionally a temperature. Steam can sometimes help with the difficulty in breathing by keeping the air passages moist and limiting any swelling. Try with a kettle gently boiling in the corner of your child's room but stay with him whilst you do this. In severe cases your child may go blue because the airway is obstructed by inflammation and he cannot get enough oxygen.

You should always immediately seek the advice of your doctor if your child has difficulty in breathing and especially if he is going blue. The doctor will probably send him to hospital. In hospital the child may well be treated inside a special plastic tent; this allows oxygen and humidity to be given. Antibiotics are occasionally used if a secondary bacterial infection is suspected. The illness lasts for varying times from hours to days and in rare cases even goes on for a week or so. Second bouts do sometimes occur.

## Bronchitis

Bronchitis is an inflammation of the larger bronchial breathing tubes; the cause is generally a virus. It occurs mainly in older children and the child is rarely very ill. The child has a cough and only occasionally a wheeze. Antibiotics are often prescribed, because of the risk of secondary bacterial infection, and cough medicines can be taken for the cough. Secondary smoking by the child (i.e. breathing in other people's cigarette smoke) can aggravate the condition. This condition does not go on to the type of chronic bronchitis seen in adults.

"Wheezy bronchitis" occurs in younger children (under 5 years); the child has a wheeze caused by air turbulence in the breathing tubes, when he has a chest cold. This is because the bronchi are inflamed and produce mucus, which obstructs the airflow. Several attacks can occur over a period of time. Although often confused with asthma, these children do not have asthma and usually grow out of the tendency to wheeze. Only rarely does it go on to true asthma. The treatment mainly involves drugs which open up the bronchi (bronchodilators) and occasionally physiotherapy.

## Bruising *(See Spontaneous Bruising on page 89)*

## Car Sickness *(See Travel Sickness on page 95)*

## Cat Scratch Fever

This is a viral illness introduced by a cat scratch, which results in local lymph gland swelling. This usually appears as tender lumps in the armpit or groin depending on the site of the scratch. The child may also have a headache, fever and generally feel unwell. There is no specific treatment, although paracetamol or aspirin will make the child feel better. The length of the illness varies. Not all cats carry the virus, nor do all cat scratches lead to it; you can't treat the cat but you don't need to get rid of it either.

## Cavernous Naevus *(See section (a) of Naevi on page 68)*

## Cheating *(See section (g) of Behaviour Disorders on page 27)*

## Chicken Pox (Varicella)

Chicken pox is caused by a virus and, except in children who have a defect in their immunity, it is generally a mild illness. It is a disease of childhood although adolescents and adults can occasionally also catch it if they missed out having it when younger. The disease is highly contagious; once one child in a class gets it, the whole class will usually become infected. Chicken pox has an incubation period of one to three weeks; the child is infectious from two days before the onset of the rash until all the spots have crusted and scabbed over. It is usual to keep the child away from school for a week or so after the onset of the rash, or until all the spots have crusted.

The rash is generally the first sign of the illness; it starts on the face and trunk. It consists of crops of small spots or vesicles which burst, become pustular and then dry over and scab. This process takes about seven days. The crops may be in different stages of development, so that vesicles are seen in some areas, while there are scabs in others. Complications, such as pneumonia, are rare in children. The most disturbing feature of the illness to the child is that the rash is itchy. Calomine lotion dabbed on to infected areas is helpful, especially the cream-based type which gives a longer-lasting coverage. Mild sedation usually with an antihistamine to help the itchiness can also be used. Paracetamol or aspirin helps if there is a fever.

## Chilblains *(See Cold Injury below)*

## Cold Injury (Frostbite, Chilblains)

Chilblains are small areas of redness, which may be painful, itchy and blister. They recur if you are not careful whenever the conditions are conducive. Make sure that your child is warmly dressed in cold weather and wears woolly socks, gloves and a hat. The cause is a local restriction of blood flow to the skin caused by the cold. Chilblains last for two to three weeks. The area should be kept warm. If they are severe, see your doctor, who may prescribe a steroid cream.

Frostbite is a more severe form of chilblain and occurs in really cold weather. The blood vessels to the skin contract; the skin can be red, white or blue depending on the amount of blood flow. The area needs to be rewarmed. In severe cases the child may need to be admitted to hospital.

## Colds *(See Coughs and Colds on page 38)*

## Colour Blindness *(See section (c) of Vision Defects on page 99)*

## Coma

Coma is the term used to describe a state of unconsciousness where it is not possible to rouse the patient even with painful stimuli. It may be caused by head injury, serious infections such as meningitis, poisoning and certain metabolic disorders such as a low blood sugar. If your child becomes comatose, lie him down with his face turned sideways and downwards, clear the mouth of any secretions and any vomit and call an ambulance immediately.

## Common Wart *(See section (a) of Warts on page 100)*

## Compulsive Behaviour *(See section (f) of Behaviour Disorders on page 26)*

## Concussion

This term is used to describe the stunned, dazed feeling and behaviour following a head injury, such as striking the head on the pavement after coming off a bicycle. The child complains of a headache, may be slightly disoriented but is conscious and easily rousable. There is no serious damage to the brain and usually no fracture on X-ray. You will be advised to report any vomiting, if the pupils are unequal (suggesting some pressure on the brain), or if your child's confusion increases and/or he becomes unrousable. The time course for full recovery is variable and may take some days; the child will prefer to stay in bed, to be quiet and possibly not wish to eat. You usually only need to give him general care.

## Congenital Defects

Any abnormality found at birth is said to be congenital in origin. Abnormalities can be minor such as a skin tag on the ear or major, such as a hole in the heart, a defective limb, dislocated hips, cleft lip or palate, an abnormality of the kidney or urinary tract and so on. The precise cause is often unknown but the possibilities include drugs or infections in early pregnancy or a chromosomal genetic defect. Most congenital defects are discovered at birth or shortly after; treatment obviously depends on the problem.

## Congenital Dislocation of the Hip

In the newborn baby the hip joint is frequently a little loose at first and tightens with time. The doctor may feel a "click" when he examines the hips but so long as the joint is stable and he is not able to dislocate it, then this is normal and the hip will develop normally. If the doctor is unsure of the stability of the joint, he might recommend that you use "double nappies" (it is best to use two terry towelling nappies) to act as a sort of splint and that you nurse your baby on his tummy. Then he will recheck the hips at two to three months. If the hip joints are frankly dislocated (that is, one bone easily separated from the other) proper splinting by an orthopaedic surgeon is required. What one wishes to avoid is the minor risk of permanent damage to the hip joints and later problems with walking. Splinting is often required for many months to allow the joint to develop properly. Most clicks disappear with this treatment.

## Conjunctivitis

Conjunctivitis is one of the causes of a red eye, where the outer membrane lining of the eye and the inside surfaces of the lids are inflamed. There may be a whitish or yellow discharge and the eye feels painful and gritty. The child may complain that the eyes feel stuck together first thing in the morning. Conjunctivitis can occur at any age; the cause is either bacterial or viral infection or it may be due to chronic irritation by a dust particle or an inturned eye lash. Both eyes are usually involved; if only one eye is affected then an irritant foreign body is often the cause. Conjunctivitis is only rarely infectious from one person to another.

To treat conjunctivitis the eyes should be kept clean by regular washing with plain warm water, or a weak salt solution (see page 122). This can be done by pouring the water over the eyes (with the child's head over a sink) or by the use of an eye bath, which has the same effect. In the younger child and infant moist cotton wool gently wiped over the eyes is adequate. If the doctor suspects a bacterial infection, then he will prescribe an antibiotic in the form of either drops or ointment. In a baby, conjunctivitis can occur in a mild or a severe form and is known as a "sticky eye". The treatment is the same.

## Constant Catarrh *(See Running Nose on page 81)*

## Constipation *(See also page 153)*

The word constipation means different things to different people; to the doctor it means the passage of hard and infrequent stools. The word infrequent is also open to different definitions in this context; some people expect to open their bowels every day, others only once a week. The latter does not itself amount to constipation. Provided the child feels well, behaves normally, has no pain and his tummy feels soft, he is not truly constipated, so do not worry if he has not had his bowels open for a couple of days. If there is discomfort on passing the stool and it is hard and dry, then he is constipated. Simple measures usually work: fruit juice, a little brown sugar added to the formula if the infant is not yet weaned, bran, all do wonders. Laxatives or stool softeners should be held in reserve and only used as a last resort or if there is a medical reason for doing so.

Occasionally the child holds back his stool for fear of pain, for example, when there is a small tear in the skin around the anus (an anal fissure). In this case stool softeners help make going to the toilet more comfortable, so that the raw area is not further irritated by a hard stool. Severe constipation in a newborn baby may be due to a medical illness, such as a poorly functioning thyroid gland or an illness of the lower bowel called Hirschprungs disease. In general, however, making a fuss over bowel motions usually makes things worse.

## Convulsions (Seizures, Fits)

Not all convulsions are due to epilepsy. A convulsion is caused by abnormal electrical activity in the brain which is then translated into excessive, rapid, muscle activity, so that the limbs are moved jerkily and involuntarily. There is often an associated loss of consciousness, of memory and of control of bowel and bladder function. There are many causes. These include high fever, an infection of the brain, such as meningitis, a metabolic disorder, such as low blood sugar, and certain drugs. Sometimes convulsions follow damage to the brain which has occurred at around the time of birth. A convulsion, regardless of the cause, may be generalized or major (grand-mal) involving the whole body, focal involving only part of the body, such as a limb, or minor (petit-mal), as described below. What you should do if your child has a convulsion due to a fever at home is described on page 120. Treatment of a convulsion involves several steps: firstly drugs to stop an on-going acute convulsion, next investigation and treatment of the cause and then possibly even long-term anti-convulsant drugs to prevent recurrences are given.

## (a) *Infantile Spasms* (Salaam Seizures, Hypsarrythmia)

These are recurrent seizures which can affect a child usually in the first year of life. There may be many in a day. The onset is sudden, with short, rapid, repeated episodes of the child curling up and flexing his whole body, which then relaxes. There may also be a short cry but the child does not appear to be in pain. The infant stops developing normally. This is a serious disorder with a major risk of later mental retardation. Early diagnosis and treatment (with drugs) is important. The cause is unknown.

## (b) *Febrile Convulsions*

This type of convulsion is extremely common. It occurs between the ages of six months and five years and is associated with a rapid rise in body temperature; the temperature can be due to any cause, such as a middle ear infection or even measles. The child's brain is irritated by the increase or change in temperature causing a discharge of electrical activity, the end result of which is a generalized convulsion. It can last for one second or go on for minutes. At the end of the convulsion the child may be semi-conscious or go into a deep sleep. You should lie the child with his face sideways and down and not restrain him. Then seek medical help.

The treatment of this convulsion is the same as for any other cause, namely anti-convulsant drugs. The doctor will then seek the reason for the temperature and treat this specifically, for example with antibiotics, if it is due to a middle ear infection, as well as prescribing treatment to bring the temperature down. With the first febrile convulsion, many doctors recommend a routine lumbar puncture (a tap of the spinal fluid, which is generally done in hospital), as it is often very difficult to be sure that the cause is not due to a brain infection (meningitis).

Once it has been established that the convulsion was due to a rapid rise in temperature alone, you will be given advice as to what steps to take next time the child has a high temperature and how to bring this down in order to prevent a recurrence of the convulsions. Usually a drug such as paracetamol or aspirin is recommended, as is tepid sponging (see page 120). These convulsions do not go on to cause either brain damage or future epilepsy. There is controversy, however, as to whether children who have more than one febrile convulsion or whose initial convulsion or subsequent convulsions are particularly pro- longed, should be put on regular anti-convulsant drugs until the age of five or older. Medical opinion still varies on this question.

## (c) *Epilepsy*

Epilepsy has been known about for centuries; Julius Caesar was said to have suffered from it. It is a disease of the brain and nervous system resulting in disordered electrical activity of the brain. Mental ability is usually not affected. The causes are various but there is often a family history and some forms are indeed inherited. An example of the inherited form is epiloia (tuberous sclerosis). There are many causes of convulsions, particularly in the newborn baby and younger child, which do not develop into epilepsy.

Whatever the form, two types of disease are recognized, grand-mal and petit-mal. These terms refer to the type of convulsion and also to the electrical pattern recorded on an electroencephalogram (EEG). In grand-mal epilepsy the child has major seizures. There is frequent loss of consciousness, loss of memory and loss of bowel and bladder control. There may be warning symptoms, such as spots in front of the eyes or strange sounds and smells. Drugs may abort the attack; the long-term taking of anti-convulsant medicine should limit the number of attacks. These medicines do not treat the cause but only suppress the tendency to seizures. Petit-mal or minor epilepsy, on the other hand, merely involves lapses in attention which usually last for seconds or "drop attacks" when an activity abruptly ceases. There may be several attacks a day. Petit-mal disease tends to be blamed for many childhood physical and behavioural problems; one must have EEG confirmation to be sure. Again drug treatment is available.

Children with epilepsy have special needs. Although they should not be over-protected, certain activities, such as swimming and climbing trees or ladders, should be supervised. Individual risks need to be assessed and provision made. A child should not be allowed to become over-tired, to become hungry or, when older, to take alcohol to excess, as these may trigger a convulsion. Flashing lights, such as strobe lighting in discotheques, can also trigger attacks in some children and it is probably better if epileptic children avoid these. Consideration needs to be given to road safety and whether it is safe for the child to have a bicycle or later to drive a car. The special circumstances of the epileptic may also influence the type of vocational training he should undergo at school, as certain jobs may well be closed to him. Epileptic children should attend normal schools and be regarded as normal children but with a problem. There is the risk that the child will not achieve his full potential at school, however, possibly due to the fact that sub-clinical (or lesser) convulsions are not being recognized or because the drug therapy itself is causing the child to perform below par, by interfering with concentration and attention. Treatment is often necessary for life; some children, however, seem to grow out of their illness by adolescence and have only few attacks, if any at all, by the time they reach adulthood. The long-term use of anti-convulsant drugs sometimes causes problems such as dizziness, gum swelling, vomiting, allergic reactions; your doctor will advise you about what to expect. Society's attitude to the disease is changing, these children are no longer regarded as abnormal.

## Cot Death (Sudden Infant Death Syndrome or SIDS)

This is a major cause of death in the first year of life. Characteristically a well baby is put to bed at night but is found to be dead in the morning. No cause is known for this unfortunate illness. Many theories have been proposed and these include an infection, a nervous system disability, heart arrythmia, or possibly even an allergic response to milk which has been regurgitated into the throat. SIDS is totally unpredictable and occurs in infants from across the social spectrum. Cot death is, however, much less common in the baby who has been breast-fed. No guilt or blame can possibly be placed on parents who have suffered a loss in this way.

## Coughs and Colds

A cough can be caused by a problem at any level in the breathing passages from the nose down to the chest. When there are excessive secretions in the breathing passages, these stimulate a reflex producing a cough; if the cough brings these secretions up it is known as a "productive cough". These secretions may be caused by an infection, some irritant or an allergy. The type of cough often suggests the cause, for example, the child who wakes up first thing in the morning with a cough often has a post-nasal drip. This is when the secretions come from the nose, trickle down the back of the throat where they pool during the night, causing a cough when the child stirs. Treatment may involve the use of a nasal decongestant to unblock and dry the nose rather than a cough suppressant. Sometimes, however, a cough can be a good thing, for example, if a child is having an acute attack of asthma or has pneumonia, the cough reflex helps clear the chest by removing infected or excess secretions. For this reason, it is not always wise to use a chemical cough suppressant.

The 'common' cold is usually due to a virus. The child has a seemingly continual running nose, may have a cough (often at night) and an earache. Occasionally, there is also a mild fever. The child may look miserable but is usually not unwell; the best thing is to do nothing and let it run its course. Nose drops (to be used carefully – these can be obtained from your doctor or the chemist) can be given to a small infant if feeding is interfered with.

## Cradle Cap (Baby Dandruff, Scurf, Scalp Seborrhoea)

Cradle cap is a common problem in young infants and consists of small areas of yellowish scalp discoloration and crusting. Any area of the scalp can be affected. It occurs even in babies who have their hair and scalps washed regularly. It is most common over the fontanelle (soft spot) area as parents are reluctant to wash and brush the hair there because they fear they will damage the brain underneath, although this just does not happen. The cause of cradle cap is excess scalp grease together with insufficient scalp stimulation (for example, by not enough washing and brushing). In some rare instances, the area becomes inflamed, and is then known as seborrhoeic dermatitis. The area of inflammation may spread over the forehead and down behind the ears. Once cradle cap is established it is difficult to dislodge. Treatment involves regular shampooing with medicated soap (you do not need a prescription) and then vigorous brushing and combing of the affected areas with a soft brush. Cradle cap is rarely a problem after the first few months. Treatment of seborrhoeic dermatitis is essentially the same.

## Crooked Teeth

You need to look after both the first and second set of teeth (see page 141). If dental care of the first set is poor, then there may be problems with later teeth, which may come out crooked or there may be overcrowding. Your dentist will advise you whether teeth need to be removed to make room for others or whether a brace is necessary to straighten the crooked teeth. He will be concerned not only how the teeth look (a pretty smile is not helped by ugly teeth), but also how they function at biting and chewing.

## Cross Eyes *(See Squint on page 89)*

## Croup

This is very common and is a form of laryngitis in a small child. There is a brassy cough, noisy breathing and often a fever. The cause is usually a virus. Croup is often distressing for the child, who may have considerable difficulty breathing, and the parent who feels so helpless. In bad cases the child may have real trouble getting enough oxygen and might go blue. It is always worthwhile having a child with croup seen by a doctor. If the symptoms are mild, the child can be treated at home; humidity helps and all you need to do is keep a kettle gently boiling near the infant. Careful watch should be kept on this set-up to avoid an accident. Massaging or slapping the child's back does not help. If the croup is a little more severe, then your child may need to go to hospital. The doctors there may use a croup tent to provide humidity and a little oxygen if necessary. The duration of the symptoms vary but in general they only last for a few days. Recurrent attacks do occur; each time, unfortunately, you need to start all over again.

## Crying

Not all babies are placid and the amount of crying varies from one baby to another. Crying is the only means of communication with the world that the baby has. Mothers soon learn to tell the difference between the cry for food or company, and the cry of discomfort (e.g. wet nappy) and pain. A change in the pattern of crying or persistent crying, with difficulty in consoling the baby, can be worrying. Teething, earache, tummy ache and so on, can all cause persistent crying and irritability. If you are worried, ask your health visitor or doctor to have a look at your child.

## Cuts and Grazes

These are generally due either to a fall or to some accident. Common sites include the hands, knees and the head. If there is a lot of bleeding, it needs to be controlled. It will usually stop if you apply simple pressure at the bleeding site. If, however, the bleeding is arterial and spurts and does not respond to pressure, then a tourniquet applied to the limb above the injured site may be required (see page 181). Call an ambulance immediately as hospital treatment is almost certainly needed if a tourniquet is required.

Wide gaping wounds may need stitches; any gaping wounds on the face and head should be seen by a doctor, so that they can be stitched if necessary, in order to prevent an ugly scar forming. Most wounds, however, require only simple cleaning; the wound should be washed with either plain water or mild soapy water and then with a gentle disinfectant. This should wash out any dirt, but if you think there might still be a foreign body in the wound, then ask for your doctor's advice. Most grazes can be left exposed to air, although it is often worthwhile putting on a soft dressing or bandage in order to prevent further injury to the graze area. Children seem to enjoy having bandages on them and this has an added advantage of teaching them about wounds and hygiene. A vaccination of tetanus toxoid may be needed if the wound was caused by a rusty object or if your child's immunization against tetanus is not up-to-date (see page 144).

## Cyanosis (Blue Attacks)

A child who goes blue, particularly if he has breathing problems, is a cause for concern regardless of his age. Cyanosis usually means a shortage of blood oxygen or an inadequate circulation. The cause can be an abnormality or disease of the heart, circulation or lungs. With persistent blueness call your doctor immediately or go to a hospital casualty department.

There are two circumstances which are not worrying. Firstly in cold weather it is common for the hands, lips or other exposed parts to go blue; once they are warmed, the blueness goes. Secondly in breath holding attacks (see page 26) the child may hold his breath long enough to go blue – he pinks up with his first cry.

## Cystic Fibrosis

Cystic fibrosis is an inherited condition in which there is a high incidence of lung disease, lung infection and a failure to absorb nutrients properly. These symptoms result in a failure to thrive. The condition can be diagnosed at an early stage, many hospitals do a screening test for it at birth, and with proper treatment the quality of life and life expectancy of children with cystic fibrosis can be improved.

The treatment involves regular physiotherapy, early treatment of infection and medicines to correct the malabsorption defect. The gene leading to the condition is common in the community. If two people who have the gene marry, then they have a 1 in 4 risk of having an affected child. There is no way of knowing if you have the gene unless you already have an affected child.

## Diabetes

Diabetes is a disease in which the body has difficulty metaboliz-
ing sugars (carbohydrates) because of a deficiency of a hormone
(insulin) formed in the pancreas. Diabetes can strike at any age
group. The child complains of increasing thirst and the frequent
passing of urine. He occasionally may need to get up at night or
may wet the bed. There is also often a loss of weight. Faced with
these symptoms your doctor will test the child's urine and, if it
contains sugar, will arrange for blood tests and probably a
hospital assessment.

The treatment of diabetes involves careful control of the
carbohydrate content of the diet and often daily insulin injections. The parent will need to learn about the illness, its
complications and how to give the injections. Two common
problems are low blood sugar (hypoglycaemia) and high blood
sugar (hyperglycaemia); with the former the child feels dizzy
and faint, while with the latter he feels unwell and nauseous.
The child usually learns quickly how to tell the difference. With
hypoglycaemia the child needs to be given some sugar, a sweet
or soft drink is often enough, while with hyperglycaemia an
adjustment of the insulin dose or diet is often necessary. The
illness is chronic and daily testing of urine is necessary to check
the insulin dose. Regular medical check-ups are needed.

The emotional needs of the child are important. He must not
be made to feel different and an outcast.

## Diaper Rash (See Nappy Rash on page 70)

## Diarrhoea *(See also Gastroenteritis on page 50)*

What is diarrhoea, like constipation, is a matter of definition. To a doctor the term means frequent passing of watery stools, which contain little or no formed stool. The danger is that the child will become dehydrated; regardless of the cause of diarrhoea, it is important that he continue to drink fluids. Do not worry that he does not eat. There are many causes: infection (gastroenteritis), intolerance of a food stuff, such as sugar, or an allergic reaction such as to milk, food poisoning, and occasionally as part of another illness such as otitis media (see page 66).

Drugs against diarrhoea should, on the whole, be avoided, as they do not treat the cause or aid in the diagnosis. They give a false sense of security. It is more important that you keep up the fluids; clear fluids, such as decarbonated (flat) soft drinks or proprietary electrolyte solutions, are best, milk in the young baby is then slowly reintroduced. If it is a question of a food intolerance or allergy, your doctor may prescribe a special diet or do tests to find the cause.

## The Different Child *(See section (h) of Behaviour Disorders on page 27)*

## Dirt Eating *(See Pica on page 75)*

## Dislocated Joints

Occasionally the shoulder or elbow become dislocated, for example when the elbow is yanked in one direction, whilst the child is attempting to go in another. Although painful and distressing, provided there is no associated break in the bones, both dislocations are easily corrected. Put the arm in a sling (see page 181) and take your child to the nearest casualty department. They may do an X-ray to make sure there is no break and if there is not the joint will usually be manipulated.

## Dislocation of the Hip, Congenital *(See Congenital Dislocation of the Hip on page 33)*

**Dysentery** *(See Gastroenteritis on page 50)*

**Dyslexia** *(See section (b) of School Failure on page 83)*

## Ear Ache

This is pain in the region of the ear. It can affect children at any age. The ear, however, may not be the source of the pain. It may, in fact, be coming from either the teeth, the jaw, the skin around the ear or even the mastoid bone. It is often difficult to be sure where the pain is coming from unless you look and find an inflamed area. The most frequent cause, however, is an infection of the ear itself. To deal with the ear ache one needs to be sure of the source of the pain, so that specific treatment can be given. Local treatment with warmth (such as a hot water bottle or burying the ear in a comfortable pillow) or analgesia (such as paracetamol or aspirin) is helpful to ease the pain. If simple measures do not work, see your doctor; if the cause is, for example, a middle ear infection, he will prescribe antibiotics.

## Eczema, Infantile (Atopic)

Much to the parents' frustration, it is not always possible for the doctor to make a specific diagnosis with a skin rash. Many diseases can cause similar rashes. Eczema, however, is relatively specific. This rash often starts when the infant is only two to three months old and usually affects children who come from families with a history of allergies. The skin lesions are rough, red and scaly. The child often scratches the area, which oozes, then becomes infected and looks rather nasty. The rash usually affects the face, cheeks, forehead and the skin creases of the elbows and knees. The child is often irritable; his sleep may be disturbed and his general behaviour affected.

Eczema is usually due to an allergy. This may be to some substance in his food, such as cow's milk protein (it is rare in breast-fed babies); there is an increased risk of hay fever and asthma later on in life. There is no real medical or magic cure, the lesions generally improve with time, over the years. If certain measures are not taken, however, the rash can get noticeably worse. Finger nails should be kept short, so as to limit the damage from scratching, an emulsification cream should be added to the bath water to prevent the skin from getting "too wet" and medicated soaps should not be used. Various creams or ointments, such as coal-tar and zinc oxide paste, may be prescribed to heal and soothe, or steroid creams may be used. Steroids are probably best reserved for acute flare-ups. Certain foods may seem to make the eczema worse, if so, it may be worth leaving these out of your child's diet.

## Encopresis *(See Faecal Soiling on page 46)*

## Enuresis *(See Bed Wetting on page 22)*

## Epilepsy *(See Convulsions on page 36)*

## Epistaxis *(See Nose Bleeds on page 71)*

## Excess Hair Growth *(See Hair Growth, Excess on page 54)*

## Eyes, Swelling Around the *(See Swelling Around the Eyes on page 92)*

## Faecal Soiling (Encopresis)

If a child regularly passes stools inappropriately, not into the toilet, but rather into his pants, then this is known as encopresis or faecal soiling. Except on occasions when it is an accident, especially in the younger child just toilet trained, encopresis is a cause of concern both to the parent and doctor, and sometimes even the child. It usually has a psychological basis and the child is using it as a form of emotional expression for his feelings of rejection, jealousy and so on. Understanding and patience are the order of the day; when the cause of the tension goes, so usually does the problem. In some ways it is similar to bed wetting (see page 22).

Sometimes, however, it is due to chronic constipation and poor bowel habit and, in this case, soiling is due to leakage of stool escaping around an impacted stool mass; laxatives and an enema may be needed to clear the bowel and to regularize the child's toilet habit. Some form of emotional deprivation can lead to this situation; the child literally holds back his stool deliberately as a form of protest and impaction occurs. The treatment, then, lies in discovering the cause of the upset.

## Failure to Thrive

Failure of an infant to gain weight is a common source of worry for parents; what is of more concern is if the infant actually loses weight. Weight can be plotted against age and charts exist as to the normal expected weight for age and the ranges that are allowed. The child's weight is checked as a matter of routine at a Well Baby Clinic in his first year (see page 136). Should the infant be grossly underweight and failing to thrive developmentally, physically and socially, certain conditions will need to be considered and a specific diagnosis made. Once treatment is started, then the child will usually put on weight.

## Fainting (Vaso-vagal Attack)

Fainting is caused by a temporary upset in the normal flow of blood to the brain. The child complains of feeling whoozey in the head, a little dizzy and weak and may indeed collapse in a heap. Fainting is associated with standing for a long period, particularly if it is hot, extreme excitement and only rarely with a medical cause. A low blood sugar from missing meals can precipitate a faint. The child is not fully unconscious and is usually rousable.

If a child should feel faint, sit him down with his head between his knees  or lie him down with his feet higher than his head. Let in fresh air and offer him a sugar-containing drink. If the child seems out-for-the-count, lie him down, then gently try to rouse him by talking, a soft slap or some cold water on his face. If he is not rousable, consider some other cause and call your doctor or an ambulance.

## Febrile Convulsions *(See section (b) of Convulsions on page 35)*

## Fits *(See Convulsions on page 34)*

## Flat Feet

Flat feet, where fatty pads usually fill out the arches, are common in infants and toddlers. Nothing needs to be done about them. What is important is that the feet are symmetrical and that the joints function normally. If you draw an imaginary straight line down from the knee to the ground, it should pass through the centre of the ankle and not on either side of it, that is the foot should not be turned in or out in relation to the ankle. If the feet are not symmetrical, then minor shoe modifications may be necessary. Too much fuss is made of flat feet.

# Fleas

The common flea which bites children, and their parents, normally comes from the household pet: cat or dog. The flea injects saliva into the skin, setting up an irritation and causing small groups of weals, which the child then scratches. The bite or bites can occur anywhere on the body. Ocasionally, however, a young child (two to six years old) may have a true allergy to flea bites, in which case contact with the flea bite causes a widespread skin reaction of itchy weals and blotches, which can last for days.

Calomine lotion used over the bite will help the itching. Antihistamines are occasionally used. To get rid of the fleas, the animal, the household furniture and carpets need to be treated with a proprietary insecticide on at least two occasions, about two weeks apart. The aim of the second treatment is to kill the flea eggs, which will not have hatched at the time of the first application. The furniture needs to be carefully vacuumed before and after the powder. Make sure you follow the instructions on the insecticide packet regarding how long the powder should be left and so on. Keep the powder away from children. Fleas should be no more than a nuisance.

# Flu (Influenza)

The term flu has assumed a dustbin-like quality; any situation where there are aches and pains, temperature, headache, vomiting, is commonly called flu. This is fair enough, so long as everybody knows what is meant: the cause is usually a virus, it lasts a few days, lays the child flat, paracetamol or aspirin seem to help, it is something going around and there are no long-term consequences. This is not to be confused with a specific disease caused by the influenza virus, which can cause all of the above symptoms and usually occurs in epidemics at certain times of the year (usually winter).

# Foreign Body

A foreign body can become lodged anywhere in the body. The common sites in all children include the eye, the throat, the nose, the ear, and, in little girls, the vagina. Occasionally the foreign object has been inserted deliberately. In the ear, for example, it is not uncommon to find bits of plastic, pieces of paper, peas and other objects. The problem is trying to remove them. The first aid measures are described on pages 179–80.

Where ears are concerned, the removal should be done by a doctor. If he can reach the object with forceps, he will pluck it out or he may try to syringe the object out; if this fails the child will need to be seen in a hospital as the object may need to be removed under a general anaesthetic. Insects occasionally find their way into children's ears and cause great alarm and distress by buzzing away; a small drop of olive oil into the ear will smother and kill the insect, which can then later be removed.

Should there be a foreign body in the nose it is important not to attempt to dislodge it by violent nose blowing or probing. Generally the child will sneeze and this will help expel the object, otherwise a doctor should be asked to take it out.

If there is something in the eye, the child should be discouraged from rubbing it. The first step is to try to wash the object out using either water or some freshly made up salt solution (salt added to water just to the point of being able to taste the salt, see page 122). Pour the water into the eye with the head held slightly back; this is obviously best done over a sink or basin. If this fails, look for the object, usually a speck of dust or a dislodged eyelash, and try to dab it clear with a moist cottonwool tipped swab. Should this, too, fail then medical advice is needed, as it may be necessary to anaesthetize the eye in order to remove the object with a probe.

Foreign bodies in the vagina are also not uncommon. These often cause a nasty smelling discharge with the risk of a secondary infection. Sometimes the object has been deliberately inserted by the child; the most common foreign body, however, is a piece of thread or cotton, which has worked its way into the vagina because of inadequate washing, cleansing and drying of the area at bath time. The doctor will check there is no major object by feeling the vagina during a gentle rectal examination. The object often extrudes itself or becomes obvious. Only rarely is an examination under an anaesthetic necessary. Any infection is treated separately.

Foreign bodies in the throat are usually due to swallowed objects, such as fish or chicken bones, which have become stuck. These are best treated in a hospital and may require a general anaesthetic in order for them to be removed.

A foreign body (such as a peanut) is occasionally inhaled into the lung; this can cause shortness of breath and pneumonia. Hospital treatment is essential, as it will be necessary to remove the object surgically.

**Frenulum of the Tongue** *(See Tongue Tie on page 94)*

**Frostbite** *(See Cold Injury on page 31)*

## Gastroenteritis (Dysentery)

Gastroenteritis (or epidemic vomiting and diarrhoea) is still the leading cause of death in many underdeveloped countries. It is usually due to a virus, but bacterial causes (usually the shigella or salmonella bacteria) do occur. The child does not feel like eating or drinking and there is a real risk of dehydration which can be serious and interfere with normal blood circulation. What is important is that the child continues to drink; the parent should not be concerned that he does not eat, even for days. A useful drink is flat lemonade or cola (if the fizz remains the gas produced may make vomiting worse); these drinks contain sugar and chemicals which have been lost with the diarrhoea. If the child becomes totally apathetic and refuses any fluids then an intravenous infusion in hospital might be needed. The illness usually settles down over a number of days. No specific treatment exists for the viral causes, although antibiotics are occasionally given if a bacteria is suspected. The viruses and the bacteria are infectious; careful hand washing is important as faecal-hand-oral spread is the most common (see page 167). If shigella or salmonella bacteria have been found in the stool some form of quarantine will be advised till the bacteria are no longer present.

A common complication of gastroenteritis in the younger age groups is an intolerance of milk two to three weeks after the initial illness has settled down. This is due to damage to the gut wall chemicals by the infection. In this case you might need to give a special lactose-free milk for several weeks till this has settled down.

Gastroenteritis, which is common in the first year of life, occurs less commonly in babies who have been breast-fed.

## German Measles (Rubella)

German measles is a common childhood illness which can also affect adults. It is a significant disease when it occurs in the pregnant woman, especially in the first three months, when there is a real risk that she will produce a damaged baby. The disease has an incubation period of two to three weeks and is infectious from seven days before the rash appears to about five days afterwards. You should tell your pregnant friends that your child has German measles. It is now recommended that young girls who have not had the illness in childhood should be immunized when teenagers and before they become pregnant.

In childhood the illness is mild and starts with a general feeling of tiredness and a temperature. There is then a rash over the face, body and limbs. The rash looks like a milder version of true measles. There are enlarged lymph glands, particularly at the back of the neck, the eyes appear red, and the throat may be sore. The illness differs from measles in that there is no running nose at the beginning. Joint pains, from which adults with the disease suffer, do not occur in children. Treatment involves simple general measures, such as paracetamol or aspirin, and plenty of fluids.

## Glandular Fever (Infectious Mononucleosis)

Glandular fever is caused by a virus; it occurs world-wide and is particularly common where there is overcrowded housing and poor hygiene. It can strike just about any age group. The illness has many symptoms: a child may be tired, have general aches and pains, a headache behind the eyes, high fever, a generalized reddish rash, sore throat, and usually there are swollen lymph glands particularly in the neck. The swollen glands are not tender and this is a way of distinguishing them from the swelling which occurs with a bacterial infection of the throat. The illness can linger for weeks and often months. It is sometimes very difficult to make a diagnosis without special blood tests.

Treatment will be given to deal with the symptoms, for example, bed rest is often necessary because of the tiredness, adequate fluids and diet are important because there may be a loss of appetite and control of any temperature may be needed to make the child more comfortable. An antibiotic will be prescribed by your doctor, if your child has a secondary infection, such as a chest infection. Take care not to share cups, toothbrushes, etc., as this may be a mode of spread. The spread is by contact with infected body fluids, such as saliva; in adolescence, kissing is thought to be a common cause of cross-infection. Cross-infection in the family is usually unavoidable. You do not need to keep your child off school except when he is feeling unwell in the acute period.

## Glue Ears

This is an accumulation of fluid behind the ear drum. It generally follows an acute middle ear infection (see page 66) and is associated with a blocked eustachian tube. The eustachian tube connects the middle ear and the throat allowing drainage of secretions. Occasionally the adenoids obstruct this tube. Glue ears are often diagnosed when the child's hearing seems to be impaired after recurrent ear infections; he becomes inattentive and may have difficulty at school. Treatment involves the use of a decongestant drug, grommets (see page 66) and occasionally removal of the adenoids. The child should be discouraged from swimming and should try to keep his ears dry.

## Grand-mal (See Epilepsy on page 36)

# Growing Pains

These are second only to a headache as the commonest cause of pain in children. Growing pains, or aches, are more common in girls than boys, occur around the time of adolescence and occasionally are sufficiently severe to interfere with activity. The legs are more involved than the arms. There is, in fact, no growth related to the pain. It occurs in the limbs, occasionally near the joints, but there is no obvious cause or external symptoms, such as swelling. The pain generally occurs late in the day or in the night and sometimes wakes the child causing him to cry. Simple remedies such as rubbing the affected area, applying heat in the form of a hot water bottle and giving the appropriate dose of paracetamol or aspirin all help. The only way of diagnosing growing pains is to make sure that none of the other causes of bone and joint pain are present. The pains go with time.

# Grumbling Appendix *(See Appendicitis on page 20)*

# Gum Boil

This is the term used to describe an abscess in the tissue around a tooth. The gum is inflamed, red, extremely painful and may discharge pus. Impacted, and then infected, food deposits are often the cause, when the teeth are not brushed regularly. There may be damage to the surrounding teeth as well. The doctor or dentist will prescribe a course of antibiotics. Frequent mouth gargles help keep the area clean and analgesics (such as paracetamol or aspirin) should be given for the pain. The problem may last for days and surgical incision by a dentist may be necessary for relief.

# Haematuria *(See Blood in the Urine on page 28)*

## Hair Growth, Excess

There are several causes for children being hairy, occasionally it is a racial or family characteristic. The hair can occur just about anywhere. Sometimes it is a complication of a drug the child is taking for another condition, and in some rare cases it may be due to a hormone abnormality.

If you are concerned about any excess hair growth in your child, ask your doctor's advice.

## Hair Loss, Abnormal (Alopecia)

Some hair loss when your child's hair is combed is normal but persistent loss or loss in clumps, especially if bald patches are left, is not. There are many causes of alopecia: serious illness, skin disease affecting the scalp, infection of the scalp, metabolic defects interfering with hair growth and drugs, can all lead to a visible hair loss. The hair in general will grow back in time.

Excess tension and pulling of the hair can damage hair structure and cause it to fall out. Tight braids, ponytails, rough combing, can all lead to hair loss. Some children, and teenagers, compulsively pull and twist their hair; hair may fall out in clumps and what hair remains may be of varying length. If left alone this hair grows back but while waiting, it can be very unsightly.

One condition worth mentioning is alopecia areata. The cause for this is not known but it does seem to run in families. There is a rapid and complete loss of hair in some areas causing oval bald patches. The pattern of baldness can be bizarre. The skin underneath the hair is normal. The time course of the illness is unpredictable, although it generally gets better of its own accord and the hair grows back eventually. No treatment seems effective. It can unfortunately recur.

## Hay Fever (Allergic Rhinitis)

This is an allergic reaction to pollen, dust or animal fur. The child has red and running eyes, a continual nasal discharge, often has prolonged bouts of sneezing and in extreme cases may have a wheeze. It occurs more commonly in spring and summer and just about any aged child can be affected. There is often another family sufferer. The treatment generally involves the use of antihistamine drugs and nasal decongestants. Antihistamines can cause drowsiness and this may be a problem; newer drugs are now becoming available and may be worth trying in severe cases. If nasal decongestants are used too often they cease to be of any value. Should the hay fever seem to be always present and interfere with the child's schooling and activity, then it is sometimes worthwhile to discover the precise cause of the allergy. Skin and blood tests are carried out and treatment which desensitizes the child can be tried. The tests are usually carried out in a hospital paediatric clinic.

## Head Banging (See section (f) of Behaviour Disorders on page 27)

## Head Lice (Nits, Pediculus capitis)

Nits are most common in the preschool and young school child. They are transferred by hand and head-to-head contact. Nits are epidemic in some areas. The nit (or louse) feeds off the scalp; eggs are laid at the base of hairs. They look like small shining specks and will not brush off with ordinary combing. The nit injects saliva which causes irritation. With scratching there is a danger of a bacterial infection being introduced, causing an impetigo, which will need to be treated separately (see page 60). The whole family or school class should be treated. The doctor will prescribe a malathion lotion which is rubbed into the scalp and left overnight, then washed off the next morning. The treatment may need to be repeated in order to make sure the problem has been completely eradicated or to deal with any recurrence.

## Headache

A headache is a common complaint in childhood. There are many causes, most of them minor, but occasionally some headaches are due to serious disease. Early morning headaches or headaches combined with a reluctance to look at light are sometimes associated with serious illnesses and a doctor's advice should be sought.

Problems in the mouth, such as tooth decay, infections in the ear, sore throats, difficulties of vision (indicating a need for glasses) and psychological problems can all cause headaches. The more serious headaches usually have associated signs and symptoms, such as vomiting and confusion. Simple headaches will respond to simple remedies, such as paracetamol or aspirin, and of course specific treatment for, for example, the ear problem.

## Heart Murmur

Murmurs are noises from the heart caused by a disturbance in the flow of blood as it passes through the heart and great vessels. They are detected by means of listening to the heart through a stethoscope. The finding of a heart murmur in a child always causes anxiety to the parent, though heart murmurs are, in fact, themselves harmless and do not need any treatment. The cause of the murmur might, however, be important. Murmurs which are caused by insignificant or slight changes in flow are called innocent murmurs. These murmurs have particular characteristics and when they are picked up either at school or by your G.P., a note will be made, possibly a hospital check-up arranged but rarely will any further action be needed. The child should be treated as he was before the murmur was discovered and there is certainly no need to restrict his activity or worry excessively.

Structural defects of the heart or great vessels, such as the various forms of holes in the heart, also have murmurs associated with them. These murmurs, on the other hand, have different characteristics and are often associated with other symptoms and clinical findings. The child may be blue (cyanotic), suggesting that the circulating blood is not properly oxygenated or he may be breathless with feeding (if an infant) or with activity (if older) because the heart is failing to circulate the blood efficiently. These children generally will restrict their own activity; you should not treat them as if they were delicate but rather allow them to lead as normal a life as possible. This type of defect is, in fact, often present either at birth or shortly thereafter. Specialist advice is necessary; surgery may need to be carried out to correct the defect.

If your child has a heart murmur due to a structural change and needs dental treatment or minor surgery, your doctor might recommend that he be given antibiotics to cover the risk of bacteria entering the blood stream and settling on the damaged portion of the heart.

It should be remembered that many people go through life with heart murmurs of which they are totally unaware.

## Henoch – Schönlein Purpura *(See Purpura on page 78)*

## Hepatitis, Infectious

Hepatitis is caused by a virus. It is acquired by contact with infected body secretions. The illness is relatively rare and can be mild or serious. The first symptoms include a headache, general feeling of tiredness, nausea, loss of appetite, vomiting and abdominal pain. The stools frequently look pale. Jaundice sets in one to two weeks later. The urine becomes dark and the eyes look yellow. The diagnosis is confirmed by laboratory tests.

Children can usually be treated at home. It is important to maintain a high standard of hygiene, so that other members of the family do not become infected.

Try to avoid giving the child any drugs as these frequently need to be processed by the liver, which will not be able to cope. Protective gamma-globulin can be given to other members of the family. If the jaundice is particularly prolonged or the child very ill, he may need to be admitted to hospital for further investigation and treatment.

# Hernia

A hernia is caused by weakness in a muscle resulting in protrusion of tissue through the defect. The two most common hernias in children are an umbilical hernia, where there is a protrusion of intestine through a defect in the muscle wall around the umbilicus, and an inguinal hernia in the groin. A lump, which may gurgle when pressed, is what is usually noticed by the parent.

No treatment is necessary for an umbilical hernia. The old practice of strapping the child's abdomen after having applied a florin is unnecessary. The best thing to do is to leave the hernia alone; it usually goes by the age of five or six.

Inguinal, or groin, hernias may, however, cause trouble. The danger is that a piece of bowel may become trapped. This will cause the intestine to obstruct and may damage the bowel permanently. Inguinal hernias can occur at any age but are more common in babies. Surgery is usually advised. This can be carried out even on the smallest of babies and usually only a day or two in hospital is all that is required.

## Hip, Congenital Dislocation of the (See Congenital Dislocation of the Hip on page 33)

## Hook Worm (See section (e) of Worms on page 103)

## Hydrocephalus

In this condition the fluid pressure of the brain inside the skull is chronically increased causing the head to enlarge. The problem is usually evident shortly after birth but can occur later as a complication of meningitis. An operation to insert a special valve may be needed to relieve the pressure; the danger with excessive pressure is that the brain may be damaged. Continuous treatment for many years, and often life, is necessary.

## Hydrocoele

A hydrocoele is a collection of fluid around the testicle. The scrotum feels and looks full but is not painful. The fluid results from a failure of the normal closure of the communication between the scrotum and abdomen, which exists in the developing foetus. A hydrocoele is often evident shortly after birth. No treatment is usually required as the communication spontaneously closes, as a rule by three to four years of age. Only rarely will an operation be necessary. This is when there is an associated hernia.

## Hyperactivity (Minimal Brain Dysfunction)

The child who is always on the go, refuses to settle, requires little sleep, is unable to finish simple tasks, gets easily bored, has a low frustration threshold, is impulsive and has school difficulties due to inattentiveness and ease of distractability is thought to be "medically" hyperactive. These children often have unpredictable variations in their behaviour and activity. The problem would seem to be one of a short attention span; the brain flits from one idea to another. Although the term "minimal brain dysfunction" has been applied to this disorder, there is no obvious abnormality of the brain and no evidence of any mental retardation. On the contrary, these children are often slightly brighter than average.

Many theories have been put forward as to the cause of this problem, ranging from disturbances in psychological make-up through to disorders of brain chemistry and some form of allergic (probably to food) disease. Diets which exclude particular foods have been tried; the major recommendations involve the exclusion of artificial foodstuffs, such as colouring dyes and food additives. (This is called the Feingold Diet and is popular in North America, where this condition seems to be more prevalent.) The diets have a variable success rate; the case for using them is not proven. Some doctors will rather recommend the use of stimulant drugs.

Many children who are labelled as hyperactive, however, do not have the true medical condition but rather have common discipline and behaviour problems. Firm disciplinary limits need to be set for these children and there must be absolute consistency in approach between mother and father to prevent manipulation by the child. It is helpful to seek advice from your doctor or paediatrician when things get out of hand, especially if the behaviour is interfering with schooling.

**Hyperglycaemia** *(See Diabetes on page 42)*

**Hyperopia** *(See section (a) of Vision Defects on page 98)*

**Hypertrichosis** *(See Hair Growth, Excess on page 54)*

**Hypoglycaemia** *(See Diabetes on page 42)*

**Hypsarrythmia** *(See section (a) of Convulsions on page 35)*

## Impetigo

Impetigo is a surface bacterial infection of the skin. The most common site is the face; the source of bacteria is often another area of infection, such as a discharging ear. Impetigo usually starts as an area of redness, which then develops into pustules and blisters. It may be an add-on infection to acne (see page 17). Careful washing of the body with medicated soap is necessary to stop the impetigo spreading. The infected area can be washed with a solution of sodium bicarbonate, obtained from the chemist, and then an antibiotic cream applied; occasionally it is necessary for the child to be given antibiotics by mouth or injection.

## Infantile Acne *(See Acne on page 17)*

**Infantile (Atopic) Eczema** *(See Eczema, Infantile (Atopic) on page 44)*

**Infantile Spasms** *(See Convulsions on page 35)*

**Infectious Hepatitis** *(See Hepatitis, Infectious on page 57)*

**Infectious Mononucleosis** *(See Glandular Fever on page 51)*

**Influenza** *(See Flu on page 48)*

## Intestinal Obstruction

Intestinal obstruction is, on the whole, rarer in children than in adults; it occurs whenever there is an interference with the normal movement of the intestinal and bowel contents. The child will complain of colicky, abdominal pain, may vomit bile and fail to pass either stool or wind. He looks ill. The two common causes in childhood are an intussusception (see below) and a trapped hernia (see page 58). There are other causes which relate to structural defects of the intestine and abnormalities in its development; this type of intestinal obstruction usually occurs soon after birth. Surgery is needed to relieve the obstruction.

## Intoeing *(See Pigeon Toes on page 76)*

## Intussusception

In this condition one piece of intestine has become telescoped into another. Usually this is due to a swollen lymph gland in the gut, which is carried down the intestine with normal intestinal movement, causing the gut to turn in on itself.

The child will complain of colic-like pain, which may come and go over several hours or even days as the intussusception is developing. Between pain-bouts the child may seem to be relatively comfortable. When the obstruction is complete, the child will usually begin to vomit, he looks unwell and now the pain will be severe.

In the young infant, the diagnosis can be difficult. The onset is usually sudden and the child looks quite sick, often vomits and draws up his knees with pain. These symptoms are likely to cause you to call a doctor, who will send your child to hospital. A barium enema X-ray may be done to aid the diagnosis and by itself may correct the condition; if it does not, an operation will be needed.

# Jaundice

Jaundice is a yellow discoloration of the skin caused by a failure of the liver to clear a normally produced blood pigment (bilirubin).

In the newborn period jaundice is normal; all babies are yellow to some extent because the newborn liver is not yet fully mature. There are, however, some causes where the jaundice suggests illness, such as Rhesus blood group disease or urinary tract infection. The pigment level is checked by a simple blood test. If it climbs too high, then treatment with special lights or an exchange blood transfusion might be necessary. There is a danger of brain or hearing damage if the level is allowed to climb excessively.

Outside the newborn period jaundice is never normal! Glandular fever (see page 51) and infectious hepatitis (see page 57) are common causes.

## Knock-knees (Genu Valgum)

Knock-knees is when the child cannot put his ankles together while his knees are touching. Many children are knock-kneed as toddlers (many are the reverse, i.e. bowlegged) and grow out of it by seven to ten years. A gap of up to 7–10 centimetres (3–4 inches), depending on the age, between the inner surfaces of the ankles when the knees are together is considered normal. Orthopaedic advice should be sought if the gap is greater than this, after about three to five years of age, if only one knee is turned in or if the condition has not corrected itself by ten years of age.

## Laryngitis *(See Croup on page 39)*

## Lazy Eye *(See Squint on page 89)*

**Lisp** *(See section (a) of Speech Disorders on page 88)*

**Long Sightedness** *(See section (a) of Vision Defects on page 98)*

**Lying** *(See Behaviour Disorders on page 24)*

## Mastoiditis

In some rare cases a middle ear infection in older children can spread into the air sinuses of the mastoid bone behind the ear. The infection causes pain over the bone area and fever. The overlying skin may look inflamed and the region will be quite tender. There may also be swollen nodes in the neck. Antibiotics are used to treat mastoiditis. In the more severe cases, surgery may be necessary to clear out the pus. The possibility of mastoiditis should not be ignored as it can be a serious illness.

## Masturbation

Sexual play by small children of both sexes is normal and should not be discouraged. It is the parent, or Auntie Mabel, who has the hang-up about masturbation and not the child. Contrary to popular belief, masturbation does not lead to madness, blindness or homosexuality. The practice should not be condemned or all that will be caused is later sexual guilt. The best thing to do is disregard it.

# Measles

Measles is one of the common infectious diseases of childhood. It is caused by a virus, which has a world-wide distribution. In the United Kingdom the disease is mild; in those places where there is malnutrition the illness may be severe. It is hoped that with vaccination measles will gradually die out.

The disease is most common in the school-age child. Ten to twelve days after exposure to the virus, the child develops a runny nose and a cough, he may complain of sore eyes (conjunctivitis), vomit and have diarrhoea. He will lose his appetite, have a raised temperature, and small whitish spots can be seen in the mouth (called Koplik's spots). Soon afterwards a rash appears. The measles' rash is red and blotchy and generally starts on the face, then spreads to the body and limbs.

The child is usually kept indoors and should stay away from school for a week or so, after the onset of the rash. Treatment is given to relieve the symptoms: something for the fever (see page 118), light, palatable foods to eat and plenty to drink. Antibiotics are usually only prescribed if the doctor suspects that there is an extra infection of some sort, such as pneumonia or a middle ear infection.

# Meningitis

This is a serious infection involving the lining of the brain. Early diagnosis and treatment are necessary in order to avoid damage to the brain. The cause can be bacterial or viral.

In the small infant or baby the diagnosis can often be difficult as the child is unable to complain that he has a headache or other symptoms; he may be just unwell, vomit, refuse all feeds, have a high temperature and possibly even have a convulsion.

The older child will generally complain of a severe headache, particularly behind the eyes, and may wish to be in a dark place as light will hurt his eyes. There will also be a high fever, vomiting, possibly a convulsion, maybe a rash, his neck will feel very stiff and he will not wish to move it.

The diagnosis can only be confirmed after a lumbar puncture has been carried out and the spinal/brain fluid examined under a microscope. The diagnosis and any subsequent treatment (involving a course of antibiotics) will need to be carried out in hospital. Treatment usually lasts two to three weeks.

The child, depending on the type of meningitis, may be infectious. Again, depending on the type and cause of illness, advice will be given that the family, any immediate contacts over the last week, and school classmates take a course of preventive antibiotics. The mode of spread is usually just contact with someone carrying the bug.

## Middle Ear Infection (Otitis Media)

This is one of the most common illnesses in childhood. Some 20 per cent of all children have had an infection of the middle ear by the time they have reached five years of age. The symptoms include ear ache, headache, fever, a general unwell feeling, loss of appetite, fatigue, vomiting, slight deafness, and, if the ear drum should burst, there may be an ear discharge. The cause is either a viral or bacterial infection.

Treatment generally involves the use of aspirin or para-cetamol to relieve the pain and lower any fever, a decongestant to help drainage of infected material from the middle ear into the nose and throat through the eustachian tube and the use of antibiotics to clear the infection. A follow-up appointment after treatment is important to see that there is no residual infection, no fluid accumulation behind the ear drum and no loss of hearing. If there are repeated infections, causing progressive damage, the doctor may refer you to an ear- nose- and throat specialist, who might recommend the insertion of little plastic tubes, known as grommets, through the ear drums to aid in drainage of infected material from the ear. If grommets have been inserted, it is important that the child keeps his ears dry. Infection flourishes in moisture. Swimming is, therefore, not allowed. These tubes generally later drop out of their own accord or are removed after several symptom-free months. Chronic and recurrent middle ear infections are a common cause of mild hearing loss, therefore it is important that proper treatment is given each time or the child may have problems with speech or hearing and school.

## Minimal Brain Dysfunction (See Hyperactivity on page 59)

**Moles** *(See section (d) of Naevi on page 69)*

**Motion Sickness** *(See Travel Sickness on page 95)*

## Mouth Ulcers

These can occur in any age group and are generally caused by a virus. The herpes simplex virus, which also causes cold sores, can cause a particularly severe form. In this case the child is unwell, has a fever, his gums are inflamed and his mouth is extremely sore. He may have bad breath. Small, shallow ulcers with red, inflamed bases develop on the lips and on the mucous membrane of the mouth and gums. The child is particularly miserable.

Your doctor may suggest you give your child hydrogen peroxide mouth washes or he may paint the child's mouth with gentian violet. The child may not feel much like eating because of the discomfort this causes; it is important that you offer him lots to drink. Let him eat or drink what he feels like. If he becomes dehydrated or the ulcers are particularly extensive and severe, then it may be necessary for him to be admitted to hospital, so that fluids can be given intravenously. The hospital doctors may consider using a special anti-viral drug.

Other viruses can also cause mouth ulcers but these are usually less extensive and cause less trouble.

## Mumps

Mumps is a common viral infection in childhood. Two to four weeks after exposure to the virus the child complains of being unwell, loses his appetite, has a fever and a headache. The salivary glands in the cheeks and lower jaw become tense, painful and swollen and the mouth dry. Treatment deals with the symptoms not the cause; paracetamol or aspirin and regular mouth rinses can be used to make the child feel more comfortable. He will probably only want drinks and a little light food. He should be kept isolated until seven days after the face swelling has begun to subside. Complications, which are rare, include a mild form of meningitis, inflammation of the testes (called orchitis), and possible later hearing loss. It is controversial whether adult men who have not had mumps but have been exposed to their children with the illness, should receive a gamma-globulin injection to protect them against getting it. This is suggested because the complication rate, especially orchitis, in adult men is higher than in childhood. The child is infectious for nine days or so before the face begins to swell.

**Myopia** *(See section (a) of Vision Defects on page 98)*

## Naevi
A naevus is a skin mark, often a birth mark, which can occur on any part of the body. It may be raised, flat, any shape, may go with time or stay permanently. There are several types:

### (a) *Cavernous Naevus*
This is also often called a strawberry naevus. It is a raised, reddish lesion which blanches on pressure and is caused by a local enlargement of small blood vessels. The lesion is usually present shortly after birth, often continues to get bigger over the first six months of life and then seems to regress spontaneously over the next few years. It is best left alone. Surgery is no longer recommended even when the lesion occurs on the face.

### (b) *Stork-Mark or Bite*
Here there is a flat reddish patch over the forehead and eye lids with a similar corresponding patch at the back of the head. These naevi seem more prominent when the infant cries. The

name is derived from the myth that the marks are caused by the stork gripping unnecessarily tightly while delivering the baby. No treatment is necessary as the mark fades with time.

### (c) *Port-Wine Stain*
This is serious because it is frequently disfiguring and unsightly. It is a reddish stain of variable shape which unfortunately often occurs on the skin of the face. It does not fade with time and cosmetic creams to camouflage the lesion are often necessary. Surgery is only rarely helpful.

### (d) *Moles*
Many children are born with variable-sized brown or black moles. These are usually left alone but can be removed surgically for cosmetic and safety reasons. If moles, some of which just seem to pop up, change colour or begin to bleed, they should be examined by a doctor because of the risk that they may become malignant.

## Nails
There are various illnesses which can produce changes in finger and toe nails. Skin diseases (such as psoriasis), or a general body illness (for example, large bowel colitis or anaemia), injury to the nail and local bacterial or fungal infection may all damage the nail structure. The nail may become distorted, separated from its plate, or there may be a colour change.

### (a) *Nail Infection* (Paronychia, Whitlow)
A nail infection either at the side or the back is usually obvious. The area will be painful, tender, red and swollen. Occasionally, there may be a pus-like discharge. The causes may be bacterial, viral or fungal. With a bacterial infection, antibiotics will be given by mouth and the swelling will sometimes need to be surgically drained. A viral infection, such as a herpetic whitlow, is rare and is treated with a special anti-viral drug. Fungal infections, such as ringworm or candida albicans, are also generally rare in children. Sometimes eczema will affect the nail bed, causing uneven marks across the nail, and bacterial or fungal infection is commonly seen on top of the eczema. Nail infections in general need to be seen to by a doctor.

## (b) *Nail Biting*

Nail biting is common in school children. It is said that over half of all ten year olds have bitten or do bite their nails. It is seen as a problem by some parents, whereas others consider it normal. Some psychoanalysts claim it is a type of masturbation while thumb sucking is considered by others to be a form of nail biting, but these theories are rather difficult to accept. Nail biting is associated with worry and jealousy. The best treatment is to ignore it, since drawing attention to nail biting often only makes it worse. Girls will often give it up when told it looks ugly. Since, however, it is a clue to the fact that the child is anxious, it is worth trying to discover the underlying cause.

## Nappy Rash (Diaper Rash)

A red, spotty and occasionally painful rash in the nappy region is extremely common in infants. The cause may be a general infection, commonly due to monilia fungus (candida albicans, thrush) or a local inflammation, caused by the skin's reaction to the soap in which the nappy was washed or to ammonia, formed from urine by the breakdown of bacteria in the stool after contact with the urine.

Thrush causes a scaly, red, inflammatory and spotty rash usually covering mainly the buttocks and not involving the genital region to any great extent. It may also affect the mouth. Rashes caused by local inflammation due to ammonia usually look raw and cover a larger area including the genital region. Ammonia nappy rash is less common in the breast-fed than the bottle-fed baby because of the different type of bacteria in the gut of the breast-fed infant.

The treatment of both types of rash is essentially the same. It is important that you change your child's nappy regularly, and keep him dry so as to reduce the amount of ammonia and to shorten the time in which the skin is in contact with the irritant. Exposure to air and sun is helpful and rubber pants should be avoided. Wash the area at each nappy change, especially in the creases, and use a barrier cream such as petroleum jelly or a soothing cream such as zinc and castor oil. Local steroids should be reserved for severe cases and only used after medical advice. When thrush is suspected an anti-fungal preparation applied locally and given by mouth is recommended. If you are using terry-towelling nappies wash them in boiling water (the washing machine should be turned to the highest possible temperature) and avoid soap powders containing strong detergents and enzymes. The nappies can be pre-soaked in a disinfectant solution. Many mothers feel ashamed if their baby has a nappy rash, this is totally unnecessary!

## Nasal Speech *(See section (b) of Speech Disorders on page 88)*

## Night Terrors *(See section (c) of Sleep Problems on page 86)*

## Nightmares *(See section (b) of Sleep Problems on page 86)*

## Nits *(See Head Lice on page 55)*

## Nose Bleeds (Epistaxis)

Bleeding from the nose is common in children of all ages and is generally not severe. Only rarely is it due to a serious disease (such as a bleeding disorder). It is generally caused by a mild infection in the nose or persistent nose picking. The first aid treatment for a nose bleed is described on page 178.

Recurrent bleeding is not uncommon. An infection may be treated by using an antiseptic cream; persistent bleeding may require packing the nostril with gauze, while cautery of the mucous membranes of the nose is generally only recommended when nose bleeds are recurrent and severe. This is carried out using only a local anaesthetic. Obviously the child must also be discouraged from picking his nose.

## Obesity

Reference charts exist indicating the average and ideal weight for each sex at a particular age. If weight is excessive then this is known as obesity.

Fatness, particularly in bottle-fed babies, is common at the end of the first year of life. This generally corrects itself by the second year. It is generally true, however, that fat babies often become fat children and then fat adults. Being fat in adult life increases the risk of heart disease, raised blood pressure and diabetes. There are several causes for obesity, though the ones often quoted, such as hormonal and genetic, are in fact quite rare. The most common cause is an excessive intake of calories through over-eating. Many children are offered food as a surrogate form of love. The belief that a fat baby is a healthy baby is misguided. The only way obesity can be prevented is to encourage good nutrition and appropriate activity to burn off excess calories.

Should a small baby be overweight, paradoxically it often helps to introduce solids early, so that the infant takes in fewer calories but feels full because the food is bulkier. In the toddler and older child it is important to avoid giving them stodgy and high calorie-containing foods, such as ice cream, sweets, cakes, potato crisps, and fizzy drinks. You also run the risk of rotting their teeth with this sort of diet (see page 142).

Obesity may be identified by a health visitor, clinic or school doctor; only rarely does the child or mother complain of it. Should a child be overweight, the only effective therapy is a controlled reduction diet. These diets should be supervised by a dietitian, so that the child continues to get the right amount of nutrients, while avoiding excess calories. There is probably no place for drugs in the treatment of obesity in childhood.

## Osteomyelitis

Osteomyelitis is a serious infection of bone; any bone can be involved. It may be due to spread from another infection, such as a tooth infection spreading to the bones of the jaw, or occur out of the blue. The child may just start to refuse to use a limb, or he may complain of pain and tenderness in a particular area, feel and look unwell and have a temperature. It is important to see a doctor if your child has these symptoms, as an early diagnosis and treatment of the infection will prevent damage to bones and joints. Antibiotics are used and occasionally surgery is necessary to clean out the infected area.

## Otitis Externa *(See Outer Ear Infection below)*

## Otitis Media *(See Middle Ear Infection on page 66)*

## Outer Ear Infection (Otitis Externa)

This is a moist inflammation and infection of the outer ear canal. It is caused by physical damage, such as a foreign body in the ear, or from scratching with dirty fingers. Symptoms include itching, redness of the ear canal, pain and sometimes a discharge. Occasionally there is a small skin boil in the canal. The doctor will prescribe some drops which contain an antibiotic and in some cases a steroid or anti-fungal agent. In addition to this the parent should make sure that the outside part of the ear and the canal is kept dry.

## Over Feeding

Over feeding is a problem of the bottle-fed infant. The breast-fed infant is able to regulate his own intake, whereas the parent regulates the intake of the bottle-fed baby. The seeds of later obesity are laid in this period. It is important to give the right volume of milk and not to treat every cry with a bottle. Your health visitor and clinic can advise you.

## Pain

No parent likes to see his child in pain. Pain "somewhere" is one of the most common reasons for consulting a doctor. Pain can have different characteristics depending on the organ or structure affected; this helps the doctor decide what it is due to, how serious the cause is, whether further tests are needed, whether drugs should be used, and whether it is real or imagined. He will ask whether your child has had any other symptoms, such as vomiting, associated with the pain, whether it occurs in relation to activity and whether it stops the child from doing things he enjoys.

Pain in the ears might suggest infection; pain in the limbs and joints could mean either an infection (such as an osteomyelitis), or inflammation (arthritis), or injury; severe headache may mean migraine, or even meningitis; abdominal pain might suggest infection in the urinary tract, or some acute disturbance of digestion or the intestines.

It is common for children to complain of pain in order to attract sympathy and attention from the parent or to avoid something. The pain, even in these circumstances, is perceived by the child as real and should not be ignored. It is usually due to an underlying fear, anxiety, frustration or some problem at school. Even if you suspect the pain is psychological, it is still best to ask a doctor's opinion. He will want to exclude serious medical causes of pain before he is prepared to label the pain as psychological.

**Paronychia** *(See section (a) of Nails on page 69)*

**Pediculus Capitis** *(See Head Lice on page 55)*

**Periorbital Oedema** *(See Swelling Around the Eyes on page 92)*

**Peritonitis** *(See Appendicitis on page 20)*

## Perthes' Disease

In Perthes' disease the head of the thigh bone, where it forms part of the hip joint, is effectively destroyed. It is a not uncommon illness. The cause is unknown; it usually affects boys aged four to nine years. The illness runs a two to three year course and there is variable recovery. Pain in the hip and a limp are the usual features. Your doctor will refer you to a paediatrician or an orthopaedic surgeon for advice and treatment. Long-term rest of the joint, by the use of crutches, and bed rest is often necessary.

**Pertussis** *(See Whooping Cough on page 101)*

**Petit-mal** *(See Epilepsy on page 36)*

**Pharyngitis** *(See Tonsillitis on page 94)*

## Pica (Dirt Eating)

All children, especially preschool children, will at some time, as part of a game or out of curiosity, put dirt or dirty objects into their mouth. Children will and do eat just about anything – dirt, old plaster, paper, crayons and so on. If the habit persists and becomes established, it is known as pica. True pica is not uncommon in emotionally deprived or mentally subnormal children. The danger with pica is that the child will become poisoned; eating lead-containing paints will result in lead poisoning, which can interfere with brain development and cause anaemia. The habit of dirt eating should be actively discouraged, firmness is the order of the day. The child who is not discriminating about what he puts in his mouth runs a real risk of inadvertently poisoning himself.

## Pigeon Toes (Intoeing)

In this condition the feet are turned inwards and the child stumbles over his own feet when he begins to run. It is a normal phenomenon of growth and the child generally grows out of it by seven to ten years of age. The commonest cause is either due to a mild increase in the normal rotation of the thigh bone around the hip joint, or to a torsion of the tibia (shin bone). You should seek the advice of an orthopaedic surgeon if you think there is an abnormality of the hip joint, as suggested by pain or a limp, or if there is true inturning of the foot itself (the foot is turned in from heel to toe). If the child continually stumbles and falls over his feet, then he may need to be treated by a physiotherapist, who will probably recommend corrective exercises, which can then be done at home.

## Pin Worms *(See section (a) of Worms on page 102)*

## Plantar Wart *(See section (b) of Warts on page 100)*

## Pneumonia

Pneumonia is infection of the lungs. The cause may be either a virus or a bacteria. Segments of infected lung may collapse and become solid. With this infection, the child will have a fever, a cough, which may be productive or non-productive, his breathing may be faster than usual or he may appear to find breathing difficult and may be distressed. The child may indeed appear and feel quite unwell. Pneumonia in children occurs in all age groups but is slightly more common in the younger infant. The diagnosis may need to be confirmed by a chest X-ray. Treatment involves physiotherapy to clear the lung of infected secretions, antibiotics and treatment of the fever. The illness may last for days. Steam does not help but it is important that the child drinks to keep up his fluid reserves. Very occasionally there is a need to give extra oxygen. Those children with severe disease obviously need to be in hospital, whereas milder illness can be treated at home.

## Port Wine Stain *(See section (c) of Naevi on page 69)*

## Possetting *(See Vomiting on page 99)*

## Precocious Puberty

If signs of puberty occur in early childhood, many years before puberty is actually due, this is known as precocious puberty. These children, usually boys, but it does also happen to girls, should all be seen by a paediatrician, as there is concern that the cause may be due to a hormone-secreting tumour, which needs to be treated.

## Puberty

This can be a traumatic time (for you and your child); rapid physical changes and growth occur, together with sexual and emotional development. The age of onset varies: around ten to eleven years in girls and slightly later, around twelve years, in boys. In girls the earliest signs are usually breast enlargement, menstruation (periods), followed by growth of the pubic hair. The periods are at first irregular but soon settle into a pattern; egg formation and release (ovulation) begins after the first few cycles. In boys there is enlargement of the penis and testes, the voice deepens and ejaculation of semen (often at night) begins.

The pubertal adolescent needs to learn to cope with changes (which they don't always understand) in their sexuality, with sexual encounters, and psychological changes. Parents' attitudes, peer pressure and the prevailing general social morality all influence how an individual teenager manages. There are major and minor behavioural and social changes required in this age period, sometimes bringing with them adolescent rebellion. Counselling and advice are available through your local health clinic on these and many other problems. This time period in development needs to be handled with understanding (the parent need only recall his own adolescence!), patience and a little firmness. There are no rules which work with every child.

## Purpura

Purpura is a term used to describe discrete areas of spontaneous bleeding into the skin. Small pin-point areas are called petechiae. The cause may be due to an abnormality of platelets (i.e. the blood cells responsible for clotting), a disturbance in the blood clotting mechanism itself, or some damage to blood vessels. Any age can be affected.

There are, in fact, many causes; some serious and others not so serious. The bleeding occurs in patches, can affect any part of the body and is usually painless. If you suspect that your child has purpura, see your doctor immediately. He will carry out tests, such as blood counts, to discover the cause.

Henoch-Schönlein Purpura is a special form of the condition. In this case, there is a typical rash over the buttocks and upper thighs. The child may also complain of gut and joint symptoms; usually this involves pain but blood may be found in the stool and joint swelling occurs. The cause is a special type of allergic reaction to an infection of some sort. No treatment is usually required as it settles spontaneously. Occasionally the kidney becomes involved and this requires drug and other treatments to prevent long-term damage to kidney function.

## Pyloric Stenosis

The muscular area between the stomach and the first part of the intestine is known as the pylorus. In babies this area occasionally enlarges, causing an obstruction to the flow of food between the two areas of gut. This is known as pyloric stenosis. The obstruction occurs gradually, most often in the second to fifth week of life and more commonly in boys than in girls. When the obstruction has reached a critical point, the child starts to vomit. The vomiting is projectile and forceful and because the normal progress of food is interrupted, the child will become more and more undernourished. Your doctor will examine your baby during a feed. He will often be able to feel a small mass, which is the enlarged pylorus. Drugs may be tried but a surgical procedure is usually needed. The operation is quite simple and results in a complete cure.

## Respiratory Tract Problems *(See Coughs, Colds, Croup, Flu, Pneumonia, Running Nose)*

The respiratory tract is the overall term used to describe the ears, nose, throat, airway passages and lungs which are all inter-connected.

The term upper respiratory tract usually refers to the ear, nose, throat and larynx; the lower respiratory tract refers to the large and small bronchial tubes and the lungs.

## Rickets

Rickets is a disease of bone where there is deficiency of normal mineralization (in effect calcification) making the bone softer than normal. The child develops bow legs and wrist and ankle swellings. The bones also break easily. With treatment bone structure becomes more normal and the bowing and swellings disappear. The common cause is a deficiency of Vitamin D which is important in controlling the amount of calcium in the body. Vitamin D comes from the diet but is also formed in the skin by exposure to sunlight. Vitamin D is present in fatty foods such as meat. Treatment of rickets depends on the cause; special tests may be necessary to find out why an individual child has the illness. In the United Kingdom rickets is more common in certain population groups due to a dietary lack of Vitamin D (because of traditional diets).

## Ringworm

Ringworm is a fungal infection (and not a worm) occurring in children of all ages, which may involve the skin, hair or nails. If it involves the foot, especially the toes, it is known as athlete's foot. The skin between the toes is soft and sodden, cracked and scaly, inflamed and extremely itchy. The fungus is contagious and lives in such areas as swimming pools. It is spread from person to person when towels and combs are shared.

Ringworm on the body often produces circular lesions, typically with several circles one inside the other. This type of lesion, too, is frequently scaly, inflamed and itchy.

Diagnosis is made by being able to clinically distinguish the lesion from other rashes or by examining the area under a special light known as a Woods Light. Several ointments are available to treat the fungus, one such is Woodfields Ointment. It is applied to the lesions after they have been thoroughly washed and dried. The infection should clear up in several days. A child with ringworm should probably be kept at home until the lesions have disappeared and he should have his own towel, brush and comb.

## Roseola Infantum

This disease is thought to be caused by a virus and strikes children between the ages of six months and two years. There is first a high fever for three to four days, which then abruptly settles and a scattered, reddish, non-itchy rash appears over the body. This rash fades quickly over the next two to three days and the child feels very much better. No specific treatment is necessary, paracetamol can be used if the child feels uncomfortable with the temperature. You need not isolate your child. The temperature may, however, be sufficiently high to cause a febrile convulsion if your child is susceptible (see page 35).

## Round Worm *(See section (b) of Worms on page 102)*

## Rubella *(See German Measles on page 51)*

## Running Nose (Constant Catarrh)

This is a common complaint in the preschool and school child and generally settles by eight to ten years of age. The child's nose is continually running and he may have a morning cough due to a post-nasal drip (see page 38). Often no cause is evident but occasionally the adenoids are enlarged and there may be an associated middle ear infection (see page 66). If the problem is persistent and annoying, your doctor will sometimes recommend that the child's adenoids and/or his tonsils are taken out. This involves a short stay in hospital and several days for recuperation at home.

As an everyday measure, you could try using decongestant nose drops or liquid to dry out the mucous membranes of the nose. These decongestants are available from the doctor or can be obtained over the counter at a chemist. Do not exceed the recommended dose, as overdosage symptoms can easily occur.

## Salaam Seizures *(See section (a) of Convulsions on page 35)*

## Sarcoptes Scabiei *(See Scabies below)*

## Scabies (Sarcoptes scabiei)

Infection with the scabies mite causes an itching reaction

especially when the person infected is warm, such as at night or after a bath. There is often a reddish spotty rash particularly around the waist, thighs and between the fingers. There may be a secondary infection introduced by scratching. Small burrows can be seen in the skin. Transmission of the mite is by close contact with infected people or bed linen. Normal washing and hygiene does not dislodge the mite. The whole family needs to be treated with a specially prescribed wash which is applied for two to three nights after a normal bath. Allow the application to dry on the skin. Take care to avoid the eyes. Bed clothes should be laundered once the treatment is over.

## Scalp Seborrhoea *(See Cradle Cap on page 38)*

## Scarlet Fever

Scarlet fever is caused by one of the streptococcal group of bacteria; it follows an infection of either the skin or the throat. With the use of antibiotics this illness is now quite uncommon. The child complains of a headache, sore throat, fever, vomiting and swollen nodes in the neck. After two to three days a reddish rash develops on the face, which then spreads to the body. As the rash fades over the next two to three days, he begins to feel and look better. There may be patchy peeling of the skin. Treatment can be at home; simple measures, such as aspirin or paracetamol, make him more comfortable, while penicillin antibiotics will treat the illness specifically. The child stops being infectious after one to two days on the penicillin.

## School Failure

There are many reasons, medical and social, why a child might underachieve at school.

Once a cycle of doing poorly at school is set up it is difficult to break. The child fails to learn at a similar pace to his peers and then, rather than being encouraged and being studied to find the cause, he is criticized and put down. He then responds in a negative way by switching off completely, or becomes attention-seeking by being aggressive, destructive or by clowning about. This disruptiveness brings about further criticism and further failure. Sympathetic handling by parents and teachers is necessary, so that the child realises his full potential. Some specific causes should be looked for.

## (a) Physical and Sensory Deficits

Poor hearing, bad eyesight, speech and communication problems may all cause a child to underachieve. Deficient hearing may prevent proper listening and understanding of verbal instruction, while visual defects or problems with spatial orientation will interfere with reading, writing, and mathematics. Problems with communication include difficulty with speech and understanding and also with the ability to transfer information back. These problems should be picked up before school or at school by the school doctor, nurse or teacher.

## (b) Specific Learning Problems

There may be a problem in a specific area of learning such as numbers, writing, reading or sequencing. The term dyslexia is often used to describe children with these problems; this results from defective brain–eye–hand coordination. Words are often misread, spelling is poor, the child cannot remember numbers and so on. Remedial teaching with special techniques often helps. Dyslexia is the extreme end of a spectrum ranging from good reading, poor reading, etc., on to dyslexia. These children are not abnormal or retarded. On the contrary, the opposite is often the case, the dyslexic child may, in fact, be very bright.

## (c) Hyperactivity (See also page 59)

The child is constantly on the move and is not able to settle on one task sufficiently long to finish it, the task goes badly, he becomes frustrated and may be a class discipline problem.

## (d) Unrecognized Nervous System Disorder

If, for example, the child has undiagnosed or inadequately controlled petit-mal epilepsy (see page 36) with repeated absences and lapses of concentration it is easy to see how he might do badly at school.

## (e) Problems at Home

These can lead to a careless attitude, a dislike of school, truancy and occasionally a true phobia of school.

### (f) *Illness*

Continued absence from school because of some medical problem, e.g. asthma, can obviously interfere with normal education.

### (g) *Poor Teaching*

Not to be forgotten as a cause of a child doing badly!

A child who underachieves at school often is brought to medical attention by a concerned parent or teacher. The school may refer the child to the local education authority, school doctor or the school psychological service. A doctor will be needed first, to discover whether one of the medical causes listed is present. Once these have been eliminated a psychological cause should be looked for and appropriate counselling sought.

**Scoliosis** *(See Spine, Abnormal Curvature of on page 89)*

**Scurf** *(See Cradle Cap on page 38)*

**Seborrhoeic Dermatitis** *(See Cradle Cap on page 38)*

**Secretory Otitis Media** *(See Glue Ears on page 52)*

**Sea Sickness** *(See Travel Sickness on page 95)*

**Seizures** *(See Convulsions on page 34)*

**Short Sightedness** *(See section (a) of Vision Defects on page 98)*

**Shyness** *(See Behaviour Disorders on page 24)*

# Sinusitis

Infection and allergy affecting the sinuses occurs only in late childhood and in adolescence; the sinuses do not develop until around five to six years of age. The child usually complains of continuous stuffiness of the nose and occasionally pain and fever. Treatment generally involves using a decongestant, an antibiotic if an infection is present or an antihistamine or anti-allergic nasal spray, if the problem is allergic.

# Skin Rashes

These can be caused by many things: internal body illness, virus infection (such as measles), skin surface infection, contact allergy, reaction to drugs can all cause a rash – some typical, some atypical. The rash may be unsightly, weep, be awkwardly placed or itch. Treatment depends on the cause, although soothing lotions, such as calomine lotion, and antihistamines may help. When in doubt, see your doctor!

# Sleep Problems

Children vary in their sleep needs. The number and duration of sleep periods in any twenty-four hours vary with age, from baby through to infant, early childhood and so on. Sleep disorders are common and "normal". They may be temporary or if "allowed" to persist, become chronic.

## (a) *Irregular Night Time Pattern*

The most common problem is a failure or difficulty to establish a regular night time pattern, for example, the child who either refuses to go to sleep (may be attention-seeking) or, the one who sleeps and then gets up eager and full of beans two to three hours later wishing to play. It is important to be consistent and have a regular bedtime ritual. Children find this comforting and it offers them security. A typical approach involves, for example, having the evening meal, followed by a short period of play and then a bath and bedtime story. Delaying tactics, such as the need for an extra drink, should be discouraged. A child who wakes up wishing to play two to three hours after having gone to sleep and then comes and disturbs the parents, should be steered firmly back to his own room and bed. It is important to be consistent and calm (although this is not always possible!). Children should be discouraged from sleeping in their parents' bed, as this can lead to later behavioural problems. Sometimes, however, it is right to allow this (for short periods) as a means of providing comfort and security at stressful times.

Occasionally sleep problems are due to genuine fears and anxiety. There may be parental strife in the home, a new baby on the scene, a new school or even fear of separation from the parents. Stories about witches and goblins last thing at night often plague little minds when it is dark. The child may cry out or wish to come into the parents' bed for comfort. When fear is the problem, giving the child a good cuddle before taking him back to his own bed will do no harm. The use of a night light may help.

When the rest of the family is at the end of its tether because of continually disturbed sleep, the doctor may be approached to consider a hypnotic sedative for the affected child. It must be realised that these drugs only treat the symptoms and not the cause. Occasionally, however, in the child who has not developed a proper sleep pattern, these hypnotic drugs together with the night time routine may succeed in establishing a normal pattern. Don't despair, most of these problems settle with time.

## (b) Nightmares

Occasionally there may be true nightmares. These may take the form of a bad dream which wakes the child. He can usually remember the dream but after a little reassurance and comfort he should be able to go back to sleep. Such bad dreams are often stimulated by stories and TV programmes, they occur most commonly in children around three to four years old who have vivid imaginations. If this is the case, you should try to avoid frightening stories last thing at night.

## (c) Night Terrors

A true night terror, on the other hand, can be more worrying; the child is in a deep sleep, he awakes often confused, may be sweaty, very frightened and may scream out. When he is fully awake he will not be able to recall the content of the dream. You need to spend much more time comforting this child.

Nightmares or terrors that persist may have a psychological basis and are usually associated with strife in the home or some major stress in the child's life, such as the arrival of a new baby.

## (d) *Sleep Talking and Sleep Walking*

Sleep talking is another common problem in children. It occurs often as part of a dream and no therapy is required. Sleep walking, on the other hand, is rare in the preschool child, but does occur in the school-aged child. The cause is unknown but is often associated with periods of stress, such as examinations at school. No therapy is generally required. If you should find a child asleep and walking, direct him gently back to his own bed. Children rarely injure themselves and usually the problem has settled down by the time they reach adolescence.

Commonsense, reassurance, calmness, consistency, firmness and, above all else, patience, are the virtues of parenthood which help when your child, and therefore you, too, have a sleep disorder.

## Sleep Talking *(See section (d) of Sleep Problems above)*

## Sleep Walking *(See section (d) of Sleep Problems above)*

## Sore Throat *(See Tonsillitis on page 94)*

## Speech Delay (Late Talker)

Six to ten per cent of all children have some form of speech delay. You should be concerned if your child has no speech at two and a half years of age or if his speech is totally unintelligible by three to four years of age. Delay in talking is less of a concern, if the child's understanding is normal. It often runs in families but may be due to social deprivation, lack of stimulus (usually because parents are unaware that small children need to be talked to in order for them to develop language), a hearing deficit, and, rarely, due to mental retardation. Language delay in itself does not lead to later emotional or behavioural problems, although there is an association between delay in speech and later learning difficulties at school. Your health visitor or doctor can advise you on how best to encourage speech and will arrange for specialist advice if delay is excessive. Attendance at a preschool nursery often helps. Here the child meets up with lots of other children of his own age, will have organized play and will need and want to communicate in order to "survive".

## Speech Disorders

There are various problems associated with speaking and speech development. Most of them are minor and cure themselves in the course of time. If they persist or are severe, see your doctor. He will be able to suggest treatment or refer you for more specialist help.

### (a) *Lisp*

This is when the letter "S" is intended but a "Th" sound comes out – a lisp occurs when the tongue protrudes between the teeth during speech. Occasionally there is a partial hearing loss as well, so that the child learns the sounds incorrectly. A temporary lisp is common in children; when it is severe, speech therapy can be of help.

### (b) *Nasal Speech*

Here it seems as if the child is speaking through his nose. He will often use "B" sounds when an "M" was intended. The cause is generally due to some form of post-nasal obstruction such as enlarged adenoids. Removal of the adenoids is often helpful.

### (c) *Stutter (Stammer)*

This is a disturbance of the rhythm of speech. The child knows what to say but involuntarily repeats an individual sound or word. A temporary stammer is common in young children; they are eager to communicate but exceed their fluency and so stumble over words. This occurs in over half of the nursery school population but generally settles by the time the child is four or five. A persistent stammer is more common in boys than girls. These children tend to come from homes where the parents are authoritarian and demand high standards. Emotional tension makes the stammer worse. The child often is able to sing to himself fluently and only stammers in given situations. It is important that attention is not drawn to the defect. The listener (especially the family) must be tolerant and patient. Speech therapy is often helpful.

## Spine, Abnormal Curvature of (Scoliosis)

The spinal column down the back is normally curved front to back but not sideways; any abnormal extra curving in either direction is known as scoliosis. The cause is often unknown but occasionally it can be due to destruction, through infection, of one of the bones of the spinal column, or more usually to some imbalance of the muscles of the back persistently pulling the spine in one direction or another. Scoliosis may get progressively worse with time and can be disfiguring; in severe cases, the child may eventually have difficulty in breathing, because his chest has become distorted. The disorder is uncommon but if you notice that your child's back is not straight and looks a little crooked, then you should seek advice from your doctor, who will probably arrange for you to have it checked by an orthopaedic surgeon.

## Spontaneous Bruising/Bruising

Bruising which occurs spontaneously may be considered as an exaggerated form of purpura and should be seen to by a doctor, since it is abnormal and often indicates an underlying disease.

Ordinary bruises, however, are due to an injury causing bleeding into the skin. The skin becomes discoloured as the blood in it begins to break down and be removed by the body. The area of bruising is frequently painful, purpura or a spontaneous bruise is not. No treatment is necessary for the average bruise but a mild analgesic, such as paracetamol, can be used. Aspirin should be avoided as this might make bleeding worse. If the bruise occurs around the eye it causes what is known as a shiner or black eye. This usually settles with time over a matter of days. A cold compress may help.

## Squint (Strabismus, Lazy Eye, Cross Eyes)

Most newborn babies are cross-eyed. The cause is an imbalance in the muscular activity and co-ordination of the eyes. If the squint persists, there is a danger that it will interfere with the development of normal vision. If one or other eye continues to turn-in by six months of age, then medical advice needs to be sought. What will have to be decided is whether the squint is real or only apparent and whether it is persistent or only intermittent. It may be apparent if the child has wide skin folds at the corners of his eyes giving a false impression of a squint when he focuses. If the squint is persistent and real, your doctor will usually refer you to an ophthalmologist. He may prescribe a patch or glasses to help the child use both eyes equally or he may suggest the need for surgery to lengthen or shorten one of the eye muscles to correct the balance between the eyes.

## Stammer *(See section (c) of Speech Disorders on page 88)*

## Stealing *(See Behaviour Disorders on page 23)*

## Sticky Eye *(See Conjunctivitis on page 33)*

## Stings (Wasp, Bee Stings)

Bee and wasp stings generally cause local irritation and pain. If the sting can still be seen in the skin, it should be scraped out using a needle, which has been sterilized in a flame. Do not use tweezers or finger nails as they may squeeze the sting driving it further in. Cold water often provides immediate comfort and this can be followed by surgical spirit or calomine lotion, if available; bicarbonate of soda mouth washes may help if the sting is in the mouth. Vinegar spread over the sting area helps in wasp stings.

You should seek immediate medical advice if there is evidence of general distress, such as pain in the chest, difficulty in breathing, pallor, extreme nausea, swelling around the eyes, or if a rash appears. If the sting has occurred in the mouth there is a danger that the mucous membranes may swell, thus interfering with breathing. These symptoms are all due to an allergic reaction to the sting and drug treatment is necessary. Fatal allergic reactions to stings are rare in children.

**Stork-Marks** *(See section (b) of Naevi on page 68)*

**Strabismus** *(See Squint on page 89)*

**Strawberry Naevus** *(See section (b) of Naevi on page 68)*

**Stutter** *(See section (c) of Speech Disorders on page 88)*

## Stye

A stye is a pimple or boil involving an eye lash follicle on the edge of the eyelid. The doctor will prescribe antibiotics to treat it. These will be in the form of an ointment to be applied to the eyelid until the infection is cleared or a course of tablets to be taken by mouth. He may also remove the affected eye lash to allow the follicle to drain any pus. A stye can be sore: you can relieve the pain by giving paracetamol or aspirin, or by applying a warm compress. Cottonwool soaked in warm water and applied directly often helps. The area usually heals over several days.

## Sudden Infant Death Syndrome (SIDS) *(See Cot Death on page 37)*

## Sunburn

Young skin can be very sensitive to the sun, so take care that small children are not kept out in strong sun for too long, that they wear hats, are given lots to drink and are protected by a barrier suntan cream. The dangers of too much sun are sunburn and heat stroke. Remember, too, that cars, particularly with the windows closed, can be like ovens; young children should not be left in them while you go shopping, etc.

Sunburn is not always immediately apparent, redness appears 6 to 12 hours later, the skin becomes painful and tender and may blister. Cool water applied to the affected area helps and a mild analgesic, such as paracetamol, can be tried. Local anaesthetic creams don't help much; your doctor may consider a steroid cream in severe cases. Time, however, is the main cure.

## Swelling Around The Eyes (Periorbital Oedema)

It is important to note whether only one eye or both eyes are swollen. If only one eye is involved, the cause is generally local and may be due to either an insect bite, inflammation of one of the nearby tissues, such as a sinus, or inflammation of the eye itself. Where the cause is a bacterial infection the child feels particularly unwell, the eye is red, while the skin around it is swollen and feels hard. This is known as periorbital cellulitis. Antibiotic treatment, usually by injection first and then tablets, is necessary to prevent further spread of the infection.

Swelling of both eyes may be due either to an acute allergic reaction or to general body retention of fluid, which happens, for example, with some kidney diseases. In either case, see your doctor, so that he can prescribe the right course of treatment.

## Tape Worms *(See section (d) of Worms on page 103)*

## Teething

This is the process of teeth coming through the gums. Babies vary in their reaction to the pain of this rather prolonged process. Everything possible under the sun has been attributed to teething, including excessive crying, irritability, poor behaviour, food refusal, sleep disturbance, rashes, diarrhoea and so on. Teething is not an illness and each of these symptoms should be considered separately and possibly, or probably, attributed to another cause. If, for example, a child who is teething continues to rub his ear, he may have an associated ear infection. Children who teethe dribble saliva and this may cause a cough particularly at night and first thing in the morning. This is normal. The gum may be red and inflamed and the child may have a raised temperature. In this case it is safe to use a drug, such as paracetamol, to relieve the pain and reduce the temperature. Sedative drugs are occasionally used, as these have the additional effect of helping the baby (and parent) to sleep. Local anaesthetic creams can also be applied. Teething rings or hard fruit, such as apples, occasionally also help. Time and patience are the main cures.

## Temper Tantrums *(See Behaviour Disorders on page 25)*

## Thread Worms *(See section (a) of Worms on page 102)*

## Thrush (Monilia, Candida Albicans)

Thrush is caused by a fungus and is mainly a problem in young babies. It occurs in the mouth, where small whitish flecks on the tongue and cheek are seen. The inflammation may cause discomfort and interfere with the infant's feeding and sucking. The infection is passed on by the mother at the time of birth or from poorly sterilized bottles. Thrush can also occur in the buttocks area and cause a nappy rash. The buttock is frequently red and raw. Thrush is also occasionally seen in the vaginal area of young schoolgirls. Treatment is by use of a preparation for the mouth and a cream for the buttock or infected area (See Nappy Rash, page 70).

## Thumb-sucking

Even unborn babies in the womb suck their thumbs. Thumb-sucking provides pleasure and comfort to the child; it occurs equally in breast-fed and bottle-fed babies. It is preferable for the child to suck his thumb than to have a dummy (pacifier). He is in control when he sucks his thumb! Thumb-sucking does not damage teeth unless it persists as a habit past six to seven years. Don't get worked up about it, they all do it.

# Tongue Tie

This is not uncommon. The tongue tip is connected by a fibrous or mucous band to the muscle at the floor of the mouth, so that the child cannot completely stick his tongue out or touch his palate with it. Occasionally a tongue tie may cause speech to be slightly indistinct but on the whole it rarely causes any real problems. It does not, for example, cause feeding problems in the young child and is not a cause of speech delay. There is, therefore, very rarely any need to treat it. Most tongue ties correct themselves with time; only in the most severe of cases will your doctor recommend treatment. This should be delayed several months to see if it is really necessary and then only be done by a surgeon in hospital.

# Tonsillitis

This is a bacterial or viral infection causing inflammation of the tonsils. The tonsils are lymph nodes on either side of the back of the throat. When infected they become swollen and tender. The child complains of a sore throat, fever and feels generally unwell. You may also be able to feel tender lymph glands in the neck. Treatment involves giving the child plenty to drink and possibly a drug, such as paracetamol, for the fever. If a bacterial cause is suspected the doctor will prescribe antibiotics. If there are recurrent attacks causing a child to be frequently off school and regularly unwell, then the doctor will discuss with you whether the tonsils should be removed. This involves a short stay in hospital and an operation with a general anaesthetic.

Pharyngitis is generally due to a virus. This may cause the child to feel unwell, have a fever and also complain of a sore throat. The tonsils are not involved. Antibiotics are not ordinarily prescribed. The only measures used are those to treat the symptoms, such as regular fluids and a drug to bring down the temperature.

# Toothache

"Toothache" may be caused by tooth decay, inflammation of the gums, or by referred pain from the ear or the bones of the jaw. Tooth pain is generally due to decay and the formation of holes. These are caused by bacteria, which change sugar in food left between the teeth into acids which then attack the tooth structure. When the top coat of the tooth (the enamel) has been destroyed in this way, the nerve is exposed to any fermentation in the food stuffs, which causes pain; or there may be a collection of pus under pressure at the base of the tooth causing a painful abscess. Paracetamol or aspirin may dull the pain, cloves are said to help, but really what is needed is a dentist to carefully clean out the debris of the cavity and cover it with a filling. Occasionally antibiotics are required.

## Torsion of the Testis

This can occur at any age and involves the twisting, for some reason, of the testis on its stalk. There is sudden acute pain and the child complains of nausea and frequently vomits. There may be a slight temperature. The testis looks swollen and is extremely tender to touch. See a doctor straightaway or, better still, take the child to the hospital casualty department directly. It will need to be corrected surgically under anaesthetic; delay in treatment may cause damage to the testis leading to later loss of function and sterility. The second testis is fixed in the scrotum at the same time.

## Torticollis *(See Wry Neck on page 103)*

## Train Sickness *(See Travel Sickness below)*

## Travel Sickness (Motion, Train, Car, Sea Sickness)

Travel or motion sickness is due to a disturbance in the balance mechanism of the inner ear during movement, which in turn stimulates the vomiting centre of the brain. Travel sickness is common in the pre-school child but he generally grows out of it.

When a susceptible child is travelling (whatever the mode of travel), he becomes pale, quiet, looks unwell, may complain of feeling dizzy and vomits. It is important to try to be calm so that the vomiting pattern does not become established; apart from being distressing to most children, some may use this vomiting as attention-seeking behaviour. Travel sickness is made worse by parental anxiety and should be regarded more as an inconvenience than anything else. Simple measures like avoiding big meals before setting out on a journey, opening car or train windows for fresh air, etc., can be tried; drugs given shortly before the start of a journey can also be used. You do not need a prescription for travel sickness tablets but be sure you use them only according to the instructions on the packet.

## Tummy Pain *(See Abdominal Pain on page 16)*

## Undescended Testis

The testes develop in the abdomen of the foetus and late in fetal life gradually descend down what is known as the inguinal canal to the scrotal sac. Occasionally at birth one or both testes have not completed this descent. In over three-quarters of cases, where a doctor has difficulty feeling a testis at birth, complete descent has occurred by one year. The testis will occasionally readily return high up into the inguinal canal and therefore be difficult to feel; it can be stroked down by hand to its normal place. A high testis is a normal variant; if, however, the testis is not completely in the scrotum by three years of age, surgery to bring it down will need to be considered. Failure to bring it down may interfere with the normal development of the testis and its future function. The timing of the operation varies between surgeons but is usually performed in the pre-school age group.

# Urinary Tract Infection

Infection of the urinary tract can occur at any level – the kidneys (pyelonephritis), the ureters, the bladder (cystitis), or the urethra. Infection is more common in females than males, except in the newborn period, when it seems to be equally common in boys and girls. The symptoms include pain either locally over the kidneys or bladder or on passing urine, together with more frequent passing of urine day and night. There are often nonspecific symptoms also, such as general irritability, feeding difficulties, vomiting and diarrhoea, increased temperature, failure to thrive and bed wetting.

In order to treat the infection it first has to be confirmed. This is done by a urine test to discover any pus cells and bacteria. Once the diagnosis is confirmed, a course of antibiotics will be given, along with advice that the child should drink a lot. Sometimes there are symptoms of the infection but the test is negative. Treatment is still given. If you think your child may have a urinary tract infection, then see your doctor as soon as possible. Sometimes there is repeated infection and it might be necessary for the child to take low dose antibiotics for a prolonged period. When there has been a urinary tract infection, it is important that the urine is checked on a regular basis (this is usually done once or twice a year by your doctor) to see that there is no recurrence. With repeated infection, or for boys often with the first infection, a special X-ray of the urinary tract (called an intravenous pyelogram or urogram) is often done to make sure that there is not an abnormality of the urinary tract structure, which will make it more liable to infection.

If an abnormality is found this may need to be treated separately. The most common finding is what is known as ureteric reflux. Here there is a reversal of the normal passage of urine, so that it goes from the bladder back up the ureters and is due to defective valves in the bladder wall. These valves may have been damaged by an earlier infection. This finding is not uncommon, especially in little girls.

The risk with repeated infections, even of the bladder, is that the kidneys may become scarred and permanently damaged. It is obviously important that urinary tract infection is taken seriously and treated properly.

**Varicella** *(See Chicken Pox on page 30)*

**Vaso-vagal Attack** *(See Fainting on page 47)*

**Verruca** *(See section (b) of Warts on page 100)*

## Vision Defects

The eyes operate very much like cameras. An image is projected to the back of the eye, where it falls on the retina, which then processes this image and translates it into nervous signals. These are then interpreted as pictures by the brain. Visual problems should be suspected in children who frequently stumble into and over objects, have difficulty identifying objects, or seem to miss objects they are trying to pick up. They may also have difficulty learning to read or their eyes may tire easily. The most common defects, other than squint, are myopia, hyperopia and astigmatism. Routine eye examination should pick up these disorders.

### (a) *Myopia (Short sightedness) and Hyperopia (Long sightedness)*

If the eye ball proportions are not correct or the lens does not properly bend the light rays, the image will fall either in front of the retina (myopia or short sightedness) or behind it (hyperopia or long sightedness). Either of these two conditions limits the ability of the eye to focus. The long sighted child sees objects in the distance quite clearly but has trouble close up; the short sighted sees near objects well but cannot focus in the distance. Glasses may be needed to correct the defect.

## (b) *Astigmatism*

If the outer cornea or the lens is improperly curved causing deflection of some of the image, the retina will perceive a distorted picture. This is known as astigmatism. It can be diagnosed by giving the child a series of black lines to look at. To a child with this defect the lines will appear neither straight nor uniformly black. Glasses are needed.

## (c) *Colour Blindness*

If the child cannot perceive colours appropriately, he is said to be colour blind. Reds and greens are the usual colours involved. Colour blindness runs in families and is more common in males. It cannot be treated.

## (d) *Squints (See page 89)*

# Vomiting

Vomiting is the forceable expulsion of the stomach contents through the mouth. This should not be confused with simple regurgitation of food (possetting) which is commonly seen in young infants, particularly when they bring up wind. There are many causes of true vomiting, some insignificant but others quite important. Vomiting, for example, occurs in meningitis but it also occurs with simple ear infections. The type and severity of vomiting may suggest the cause, for example, bilious vomiting is often associated with some form of intestinal obstruction. Very rarely a child will vomit deliberately; this type of vomiting is an expression of rejection.

In most circumstances all that is important is that the child is able to keep down some liquids until the acute episode causing the vomiting has passed. With persistent vomiting, or if the child is otherwise ill, then you should see your doctor.

## Warts

Warts are caused by a virus and can occur on any part of the body. Almost all children will have a wart at some time.

### (a) *Common Wart*

Common warts may be individual or occur in crops. A common site is on the finger. It is probably best if they are left alone, as they will eventually disappear by themselves but may last months or longer. If treatment is felt necessary, a chemical paint can be used (Podophyllin) or the area can be cauterized either electrically or with carbon dioxide snow.

### (b) *Plantar Wart/Verruca*

This is a wart on the sole of the feet; it is more common in children who spend a lot of time without shoes. A plantar wart or verruca can be painful and interfere with walking. It may need to be surgically cut out after the area is painted with chemical Podophyllin. A local anaesthetic is generally used.

## Wasp Stings *(See Stings on page 90)*

## Wax

This is a common complaint. The child often has a feeling of fullness in his ear, whilst the parents complain he is inattentive and occasionally disobedient, presumably because he fails to hear certain sounds and pitches of the voice. It is important that you do not poke or attempt to pick the ear. Wax will usually come out of its own accord. Occasionally the doctor may suggest the use of oil-based drops or he may syringe the ears to remove particularly hardened wax. You should never attempt to syringe the ear at home, as there is the risk of infection behind the wax or that you will pierce the ear drum.

## Weight Gain *(See Over Feeding on page 73)*

## Weight Loss *(See Failure to Thrive on page 46)*

## Wheezy Bronchitis *(See Bronchitis on page 29)*

## Whip Worms *(See section (c) of Worms on page 102)*

## Whiteheads *(See Acne on page 17)*

## Whitlow *(See section (a) of Nails on page 69)*

## Whooping Cough (Pertussis)

Whooping cough can be a serious disease. There is a repeated spasmodic cough associated with a characteristic whoop. There are several causes of a whooping cough-like illness. Vaccination only acts against one particular type of bacteria, albeit the most common and major cause. Because of the controversy over the side effects of the vaccination (see page 145), fewer children have received it lately and therefore the illness is becoming more common. It is more severe in children under one year of age and the spasms of coughing can be so marked the child is unable to breathe properly, so that the oxygen supply in his blood is lowered and his brain may suffer permanent damage. Occasionally there is a secondary infection leading to pneumonia. The treatment of whooping cough involves the use of antibiotics. In some cases the child may be admitted to hospital, especially if there is a need for added oxygen. The illness is often prolonged and coughing bouts can last weeks or months. The cough itself is distressing and tiring, the child frequently has difficulty in sleeping. Cough suppressant medicines rarely work at all.

## Worms

There are several types of parasitic worms which live in the human intestine. Worms do not cause symptoms such as nightmares and behaviour problems; these are old wives' tales.

### (a) *Thread Worms (pin worms, enterobius vermicularis)*

Thread worms are extremely common in small children. They resemble tiny white threads of cotton. They may cause abdominal pain, nausea and diarrhoea. The worms lay eggs in the lower bowel and around the anus. These cause an itch. The child scratches himself and the eggs become embedded in the finger nails. Later they are transferred to the mouth by contact and the life cycle of the worm starts again. Occasionally the worms are seen in clothes and bedclothes.

The G.P. will make the diagnosis by putting a piece of sticky tape over the anal region, removing it, then looking at it under a microscope, where he will be able to see the worms. He will then prescribe drugs which both the affected child and other members of the family should take. A second course in two weeks time is necessary in order to catch worms in a later life cycle.

### (b) *Round Worms*

These are much less common in the United Kingdom than Thread worms, but are common in those countries where there is poor sanitation. The Round worm resembles the garden earth worm. It lives in the intestine but can penetrate the gut wall and spread to other tissues such as the liver and lungs. The symptoms that the child has depend upon the number of the worms; for example, a blockage in the intestines can occur or worms in other tissues, such as lungs and liver, can cause a cough or jaundice and pain. The diagnosis is made by finding worms or worm eggs in the stool. There is drug treatment available.

### (c) *Whip Worms*

These worms are also relatively uncommon in the United

Kingdom. In areas where raw sewage is used as fertilizer Whip worms are common. They cause mainly diarrhoea. Drug treatment is used to eradicate them.

## (d) *Tape Worm*

Tape worm infestation results from eating under-cooked food, especially pork, beef and fish. Tape worms are relatively common on the Continent. The diagnosis is usually made by seeing worm segments in the stool. Tape worms live in the intestines, where they feed off the food there even before the nutrients are digested and absorbed. This means that the child will eventually suffer from malnutrition, even though he is eating a normal, balanced diet. Drugs are used to kill the worm, which is then passed whole in the stool.

## (e) *Hook Worm*

Hook worm is a disease of the tropics and North America. Infestation causes progressive gut bleeding and anaemia. Treatment involves killing the worm with drugs and treatment of the anaemia with iron therapy.

# Wry Neck (Torticollis)

Torticollis, or wry neck as it is commonly called, is a condition in which the child involuntarily holds his head to one side or the other because of pain at the side of the head or neck. The pain can be caused by severe ear ache, swollen and tender neck lymph glands, mumps, or muscle spasm. Treatment involves manipulation by a physiotherapist, a hot compress, pain killers and an investigation of the cause, so that this, too, can be remedied.

In small children the head may be held to one side because of a small knot ($\frac{1}{2}$–1 cm or $\frac{1}{4}$–$\frac{1}{2}$ inch in diameter) in the muscle (sternomastoid tumour). This, when manipulated, usually corrects and is harmless. Your doctor will probably send you to a physiotherapist for advice on how to manipulate the area.

# PART TWO
# THE SICK CHILD

# Recognizing the sick child

It is not always easy for a parent to know when his or her child is truly ill and in need of a doctor's attention. In addition, parents worry that they will be bothering the doctor unnecessarily and that their anxiety for their child is unfounded. Although this is understandable, doctors have long been convinced that the best judge of a child's health is the parent, so be confident in your own observations and go to the doctor when you feel it necessary.

With a very small child there is an added complication in that he does not have the words to say he feels unwell or to tell you just where it hurts. In this case, you have to rely on your intuition. Often the only guide is that the child behaves differently from usual; the tear-away toddler suddenly starts moping, lying around and showing very little interest in the day-to-day goings on; the infant who previously slept regularly and cried only when he wished to be fed or changed becomes constantly irritable, difficult to feed and to console.

# What is normal?

It is, however, important for parents to recognize that their child will react differently to being unwell at different age periods; for example, you would expect a 12 year old girl to begin menstruating but vaginal bleeding in a four year old is quite abnormal and needs to be referred to a doctor. The parents also need to have an understanding of what is normal for their particular child as well as for the age group. Thus parents of children with a particular handicap need to be aware of how their child's behaviour will differ from what is normally to be expected. It is common, for example, for a child with a heart defect, such as a hole in the heart, to go blue when he exerts himself; it is quite abnormal for an otherwise normal child to do so. Also, what is typical for a child with mongolism (Down's syndrome) may not be so for a normal child. For one child a certain reaction may be healthy, for the other it will be a sign of sickness. The parents of the child with a special problem should receive advice from the doctor, health visitor or whoever is treating the child.

When a particular illness has been diagnosed, the parent should also ask the doctor what to expect as normal progress for that illness. If the child has chicken pox, for example, the parent can expect that there will be a swinging temperature and a rash. If, however, the child develops severe headaches and becomes delirious, this is not normal for simple chicken pox and may mean that a complication is setting in, so further advice needs to be sought.

# The likely symptoms

In general, the child who is unwell will no longer have a hearty appetite, may sleep more than usual, may become lazy and often develops a temperature. The temperature in itself is not a bad thing unless the child has a tendency to have what are known as febrile convulsions (see page 35). The temperature is merely a symptom of the illness, which is most likely to be an infection, and the child's body's reaction to it.

There are, however, a few symptoms which should worry parents and cause them to seek medical advice quickly. These are as follows:

**1. A gradual loss of consciousness.** This can occur over minutes, hours or, in some rare cases, even days. To start with the child may fail to recognize his parents or familiar surroundings, then become delirious or actually unconscious, so that he cannot be roused. This is a serious symptom and you should either call your doctor immediately or take the child to the nearest casualty department. There are many causes of a loss of consciousness and these include, for example, a serious infection, such as meningitis, or poisoning, or head injury.

**2. Laboured breathing.** The child seems to have difficulty in taking in breath, he may lose colour or go blue in the face; he may become confused. In this situation the problem is that he may not be getting enough oxygen when breathing in or getting rid of carbon dioxide (formed as part of normal metabolism) when breathing out. The difficulty in breathing may be due to an infection of the lung, larynx or trachea (windpipe), or some abnormality or obstruction in the breathing passages. Examples of these situations include croup, pneumonia and asthma.

**3. A convulsion.** It is not normal for a child to have convulsions (epileptics excepted). Convulsions (see also page 34) may take various forms. They may be nothing more than a continuous twitching of the arms and legs or the limbs may shake violently, the child may lose consciousness and often may lose control of bowels and urine.

**4. The suggestion of prolonged or severe pain.** Complaints of severe pain should not be ignored (see also page 74). Young children often withstand pain much more than an adult does. The clues to severe pain include continuous crying, excessive tenderness in one area, particularly if the abdomen is involved, and general irritability. Conditions such as appendicitis may show these features.

**5. Continued vomiting and diarrhoea together with a refusal to drink.** The danger of persistent vomiting and diarrhoea is that the child may lose a lot of water and become dehydrated. In severe cases his circulation will be badly affected and this is serious. The reserve supplies of blood and water in a child's system, particularly in an infant or toddler, are much smaller than in an adult's. A child, therefore, can become dehydrated quite quickly. It is important to realise what constitutes diarrhoea and what is normal (see also page 43); in the small infant the doctor will be concerned if there is an almost total absence of formed stool, so that what is being passed is largely pure liquid.

Vomiting is a common symptom, which has a variety of causes; it may occur in mild infections but is equally frequent in serious illnesses, such as meningitis, or in conditions which require surgery, such as appendicitis.

**6. Abnormal bruising and bleeding.** Nose bleeds which stop with simple treatment (see page 178) are not uncommon. Continued bleeding from the nose or from the mouth or spontaneous bleeding into the skin are, however, the sorts of emergency which require medical attention. There are many causes for abnormal bleeding, some quite minor but others are serious and it is important that these be diagnosed quickly. The problem may be that there is a lot of blood lost, with which the normal blood supply cannot keep pace, or that bleeding is into important tissues, such as the gut or the kidney. The doctor will refer these children to a hospital where tests can be performed to diagnose the problem. Bleeding into the skin can be the result of a blow causing a bruise, which is of no consequence, or may occur spontaneously if there is an abnormality of the blood clotting system (this is called purpura). A bruise shows up as a purplish-blue colour on the surface. It may be quite a small mark or cover a large area and will go through several colour changes in healing.

Purpura consists of small, usually reddish, areas scattered over the body; they are not caused by knocks or falls but occur spontaneously (see also page 78). As they may be an indication of a problem related to bleeding, they should be investigated by a doctor.

**7. A rash.** Rashes can occur in response to many stimuli and can affect the whole body or just part of it. In the younger child they are often associated with a viral infection, such as chicken pox or measles. A rash in one particular spot may be due to contact with some irritant, which has set up an allergic reaction; for example, a rash caused by touching a nettle or contact with clothes washed in strong detergent. The rash itself is not usually serious. On the one hand treatment may be required for comfort, for instance, antihistamine or calomine lotion, on the other, it may reflect a serious cause which must be diagnosed and treated. If it does not go away after a short time, consult your doctor.

To sum up, the best guide if you are worried about symptoms or altered behaviour in your child, is your own commonsense. One can never be too concerned. It is better to seek advice early rather than waiting to see what happens, so that if treatment is required, it can be started sooner rather than later. Seeking prompt advice also means that the parents' minds are put at rest. Concern is infectious and if it isn't dealt with, your agitation may well be passed on to the child who consequently becomes quite frightened. Then what should be a normal childhood event, such as chicken pox, becomes a major drama.

# Action and treatment

If you are worried about your child, your best course of action is to contact your general practitioner to seek his advice.

Unless you think the source of the trouble may be an infectious disease, go to see him at his surgery. Here he will have all the 'tools of the trade' which may be necessary to help come to the diagnosis. He can perform simple investigations, such as urine and blood tests.

If the cause of your concern is more urgent, i.e. if your child has one of the symptoms mentioned above, or if he has had a major accident or you suspect poisoning, telephone your doctor straightaway. He will either suggest a home visit or more likely arrange for the child to be seen in the local hospital.

Do not feel let down or that your concern was groundless if no specific treatment is given. It is the diagnosis which is important and treatment is not always necessary. Simple measures to help the symptoms, for instance, drugs to control a temperature, may be all that is required; if the illness is caused by a virus, for example, antibiotics should not be prescribed as they will have no effect at all. Often the parent feels that without some sort of treatment the child will become more ill; in fact the opposite may be the case and so do not put extra pressure on the doctor to do more.

In all cases it is important for both you and your child that you have the advice of a doctor whom the family trusts. The problem often arises where a deputizing doctor covers for your own and you are not sure how much you can trust his judgement. In this situation, commonsense should prevail. Most doctors will under treat rather than over treat and this is proper. If you are unhappy with the child's progress, then a second opinion can always be sought.

# The sick child at home

Coping with a sick child at home always involves a disruption of routine. An extra burden is placed on the family team; plans, such as dinner engagements or holidays, may need to be cancelled, so that other members of the family may well be hostile to the poor little fellow who is feeling rather ghastly in the upstairs bedroom. Reactions to this inconvenience are normal and should not be resented. It is, however, important that the child who is ill is protected from them as they may only make him feel much worse, particularly if he is not old enough to understand. It is equally important for other members of the family to recognize their feelings. Other children may take advantage of the situation to taunt the patient, for example by taking special toys out of the room or alternatively by becoming more demanding and jealous of the extra time you spend with the sick child. This needs to be coped with firmly.

What about the child himself? Firstly, the question of bed rest. The natural tendency of most parents when their child is unwell is to pack him off to bed. There is no place for bed rest just for the sake of it. Confining a child to bed will only increase his sense of isolation and boredom. Most children who are unwell will automatically slow down and it may be better for the child to be doing something quiet in, for example, the living room, where he can lie down on the sofa if he feels like it, but is still in the mainstream of the family life. Only in some illnesses, such as rheumatic fever, is it important to limit activity. It should be recognized that a restless child in bed uses up more energy than he does when playing quietly on the living room floor. Let him have lots of quiet games, books, stories and puzzles and possibly more television than otherwise might be allowed. The aim is to limit the demands for attention due to boredom and frustration. This then lowers the general feeling of tension in the household. Visitors will also be a good distraction, provided they do not overtire your child or that the doctor has not prohibited them and put the child into some form of home quarantine.

Secondly, there may be certain temporary behaviour changes as a result of the illness, which once you are aware of, you will be able to take in your stride; for example, it is not uncommon for the trained toddler or young child to lose control of bladder or bowel function when he is ill. Should too much of a drama be made of this, then the seed will be set for problems in the future. Discipline can be more relaxed when a child is sick. It is, however, important that the child is not over-indulged or that his routine is disturbed too much or again bad habits may be formed. Some parents, for example, allow a sick child to sleep in their room at night. This is fine within reason, so long as the

*An unwell child should not necessarily be confined to bed. Letting him play quietly in the living room with his favourite toys, where he can see what you are doing and you can keep an eye on him, is often the best arrangement for both of you.*

child understands that it is only to provide security while he is feeling unwell and when he is better, sleeping arrangements *will* revert to normal. Children who are cooped up indoors and not feeling well often become bored and difficult to handle. They will not be so ready to amuse themselves and will need more distractions than usual.

The symptoms themselves may present a problem to some parents; for example, vomiting often makes the observer/parent also want to vomit. If this is the case, try hard to keep your reaction from the child, as he will be depending on you for comfort and support. Likewise, do not be angry with the child if you have to change the bedclothes, as this will obviously be an extra upset to his feelings. Beware also of the power of suggestion and do not dwell too much on the symptoms, when talking to your child. For example, if you ask "Have you got a headache?" too often, the headache which was beginning to go will suddenly return and assume increased importance.

Now, how do you deal with the following conditions and treatments when your child is unwell?

# 1. Fever (high temperature)

The fever itself makes your child feel unwell because it raises the body temperature outside the range at which his normal metabolism works, but it is not the cause of the illness. It is, rather, one of the symptoms of illness and reflects the body's reaction to the disease. A high temperature is not bad in itself, except in the case of a child who has a tendency towards convulsions (see page 34). Monitoring the temperature by means of a thermometer is useful. It allows an assessment of the progress of the illness. If, for example, you have been taking the temperature regularly, you will be able to tell whether the temperature is continuing to climb or whether it is beginning to recede; this will tell you if the illness is still progressing or if it is getting better. The pattern of fever may also help the doctor in his diagnosis; for instance, a swinging temperature is not uncommon in a viral illness. Because the temperature is, as a rule, not bad in itself, any treatment aims merely to make a child more comfortable.

## Taking the temperature

There are two basic types of thermometer – the oral thermometer and the rectal thermometer. The difference between
them is the shape of the bulb containing the mercury. Both,
however, work on the same principle, namely, that mercury will
expand along a scale at certain temperatures and these points
are marked on the thermometer. There are also two scales in use
– the old Fahrenheit scale with the normal temperature in the
region of 98.6°F and the metric scale with the normal temperature averaging at 37°Centigrade.

There are two other instruments for taking a temperature: the
fever strip and the digital thermometer. Fever strips are specially formulated pieces of material which you place on your child's
forehead for fifteen seconds or so. They will, however, only tell
you whether or not the temperature is high and not give an
accurate reading. Digital thermometers are comparatively new
and measure temperature electronically rather than by the
mercury principle. They give you a numerical display of the
reading but are otherwise used in exactly the same way as
traditional thermometers.

If you take the temperature in the rectum you will get a higher
reading than if you took the temperature in the mouth or from
the skin (for example, under the armpit). The difference may be
as high as 1° Centigrade. So it is important, if you are taking a
series of temperature readings, that you use the same thermometer and the same site. The rectal temperature gives a truer
indication of the deep body temperature. In practice, however,
it is more appropriate, more comfortable for the child, and just
as good, to take the temperature in his mouth or from under the
arm.

Before taking the temperature, the thermometer should be
washed in soapy water or gentle disinfectant, then rinsed in
cold water. Alternatively, if you have a baby, it can be
'sterilized' in the bottle sterilizing unit. Then it should be
vigorously shaken, so that the temperature reads low before
use. To do this, hold the thermometer firmly by the opposite
end to the bulb and flick your wrist. This forces the mercury
back into the bulb. After a couple of shakes, have a look at the
thermometer. Provided that it is a couple of degrees below
normal, leave it. Do not lower it further or it will take a long time
to reach the real temperature of your child's body and if you

It does not matter whether you use a Fahrenheit or a Centigrade thermometer; only the numbers change, not the significance. Normal body temperature is 98.6° Fahrenheit or 37° Centigrade. A temperature does not tell you the cause of the problem, nor is it the problem! Taking a child's temperature during an illness will, however, tell you something about its progress.

The fever strip is a novel and quick way of checking a child's temperature. It is placed on a child's forehead for a short time (about fifteen seconds usually) and then, depending on the type, may tell you by a colour change either the temperature in whole degrees Fahrenheit or only indicate whether it is normal or raised.

remove it too soon you may have an inaccurate reading. The thermometer should be left in place for half to one minute.

If your child has a blocked nose, and therefore is breathing through his mouth, or has recently had a hot drink, the temperature recorded in the mouth may be higher than it should be. In addition, the temperature recorded may vary not only with the illness but also with the time of day. There are normal swings of temperature during the day; it is often higher in the evening than in the morning. It will also vary according to the outside temperature and to the child's activity. It will obviously be higher or lower according to the weather and it will be higher if your child has been running around or is excited in some way.

## In the mouth

You can take the temperature in the mouth with older children (around eight to ten years plus), when they will understand that they have to keep still and not chew the end of the thermometer. The danger with a younger child is that he may cut his mouth, swallow glass or swallow the mercury. Ideally the thermometer should be placed under the tongue, but in the slightly younger child, it is not unreasonable to place it between the teeth and the cheek, which will be easier for the child.

## Under the arm

For this method you tuck the thermometer in your child's armpit, next to his skin and keep his arm against his body while the thermometer is in place. You may need to keep it there a few moments longer than for the other methods to get a real reading.

## In the rectum

This method can be used for the toddler and young infant; it is not ideal for parents to take the temperature this way, the other sites are just as reliable. If you do, you need to feel quite confident and will probably need another adult to help. First lubricate the bulb of the thermometer with a little petroleum jelly. Then place your child face downwards on a bed or on your

Each time a thermometer is used it should first be washed in soapy water or mild disinfectant.

Then it should be rinsed clean under running water. The water must not be hot.

Finally, you should shake it with a quick flick of the wrist, so that it reads low before use.

### In the mouth
Place the thermometer either under the tongue, as shown here, or between the teeth and cheek. Tell the child not to bite or chew on it as it may break.

### Under the arm
Tuck the thermometer under your child's arm. Hold it in position for a few moments longer than for other methods to make sure the temperature records. Remember that the reading will be a little lower than if it had been taken in the mouth.

lap. With one hand open out the buttocks and with the other, place the thermometer in the rectum, so that it only goes in about a quarter of an inch (half to one centimetre). The other person can help here in keeping the child still, as he may struggle. It is important not to push the thermometer in too far or be rough, as there is a danger that it might perforate the lower gut, but this is exceedingly uncommon.

Whichever method you choose, make sure you do the same thing next time you take the temperature. This is the only way you can tell if there has been a real change.

## Lowering the temperature

If the temperature is high (greater than 38°C/101°F) you may wish to bring it down. This may be achieved by taking off all your child's clothes, leaving him uncovered and giving him plenty of cold drinks. This does not mean that the child should be exposed to a draught. He should be in a room of average temperature, but preferably not one which is artificially heated. Junior aspirin or paracetamol will also bring down his temperature but take care that the appropriate dose for age is given and that the drug is not used too frequently. These drugs when used appropriately are safe, but are harmful if more than the recommended amount is given.

For *paracetamol* the dose for a child of less than one year of age is between 60 and 120 milligrams per dose and after one year of age 120 milligrams per dose, given every four to six hours. You should read the instructions on the bottle carefully. If it is in liquid form, the dose there is often described in terms of volume which may be given either by dropper or spoon, for example 5 millilitres (equal to one ordinary teaspoon) contains the equivalent of 120 milligrams and so on.

*Aspirin* should not be used for an infant under one year as it is easy to give too much and this may then interfere with the child's ability to breathe. In the one to two year age group, 75 milligrams every six hours is an appropriate dose and this is roughly equivalent to one Junior Aspirin. In the two to five year age group 150 milligrams can be given and over five as much as 225 milligrams. This compares with an adult dose of between 300 and 600 milligrams.

If the temperature climbs even higher, for example up to 39°C/

Paracetamol or aspirin, given in the appropriate dose (see page 118), can be used to bring down a high temperature. Paracetamol comes in either liquid or tablet form, whereas aspirin is only available as tablets. Tablets can be crushed in water if necessary.

A tepid sponge bath can be useful to bring down a high temperature and make a child comfortable by washing off caked-on sweat. This should be done either on a water-proof sheet or in an empty bath. Use only lukewarm water and sponge the child all over.

103°F and especially if the child is at risk of a febrile convulsion, then a tepid sponge bath may be required. Do this in a room where the heat has been turned off but which is free of draughts. It can be done in either an empty bath or on a waterproof sheet and you will need a container with some lukewarm, but not cold, water and a sponge or cloth. Remove all clothes. Wet the sponge in the lukewarm water, then gently sponge your child all over. As the water evaporates in the normal way from the skin surface it will cool the child. If you also give your child ice-cold drinks at regular intervals, this will be an added help in bringing his temperature down.

# 2. Giving medicines

Not all medicines are designed to cure specific diseases; some are merely given to control the symptoms and make the patient more comfortable. As, for example, the use of paracetamol or aspirin described above. They will bring down a high temperature but have no effect on the infection which may have caused it. Sometimes a medicine is used more for the parent than for the child himself; a bad cough, for instance, may be more irritating to other members of the family, because it keeps them awake at night, than it is for the child with the cough who manages to sleep through it. In this circumstance the use of cough medicine is to help other members of the family to cope. The cough itself may in fact be good for the child, as in the case of a chest infection, where it will help to clear the lungs.

The parent should also realise that antibiotics are not a cure-all and have no particular magic attached to them. They are of use only in specific bacterial infections and have no place in the treatment of viral disease. It is common, however, for the doctor to use antibiotics when it is not possible, without special tests, to be sure whether the infection, such as a sore throat, is bacterial or viral. Here the use of antibiotics is merely a precaution against a bacterial infection, which may sometimes occur on top of a viral infection. Still it is not always appropriate for antibiotics to be given and you should not pressurize the doctor into giving medicine, if he does not feel it is justified. Occasionally, more harm comes out of the use of a medicine than good;

some antibiotics, for example, can cause diarrhoea.

When a medicine has been prescribed for your child there are a number of things which you should know about it. You should know its name and what effect it is intended for it to have. You should be told how to tell if it is working and what to do if it appears not to be working, whether it should be taken before, after or with meals, what to do if a dose has been missed, how long the course of treatment is and how to recognize any side effects. Your doctor and pharmacist should give you this information. It is then up to you to check the instructions on the bottle to see that you use the correct dose and that you complete the course. Make sure that when you are finished with the medicine, the top (preferably child resistant) is properly placed back on the bottle, so that other children in the family will not take it by mistake. All medicines should be kept in a locked cabinet so that they are out of reach. If your child refuses to take the medicine, do not force him. If you hold his nose and force him to swallow the substance, it will only increase his resistance and possible aggression. He may choose to vomit it back! He will soon learn to use the taking of the medicine as a weapon and means of getting further attention.

When the course is finished, discard any remaining medicine; avoid the temptation to use any left over at a later date. It may have lost its potency or you may make the wrong diagnosis.

## Tablets and liquids

Few children under the age of five can swallow a tablet whole, so break it in half, or in quarters. If your child still cannot take it, then crush up the tablet and mix it into a spoonful of his normal food. For the younger age group, the medicine will often be in the form of a liquid. Where the dose is refused, it may be necessary to trick the patient by hiding the medicine in either fruit juice, jam or food.

Each parent will have to design his own way of fooling his child if the need arises. If your child is taking a course of liquid medicines, take extra care over cleaning his teeth, since most come in a sugar form or need to be hidden in something sweet in order to persuade the child to take them and this can cause tooth decay. This is, in fact, a particular problem in children obliged to take medicines on a regular basis.

## Eye, nose and ear drops

Sometimes it is necessary to administer medicines to a particular area of the body, for example, into the eye, ear or nose or on to the skin. If you are using eye drops or eye ointments, take care not to frighten your child by approaching too rapidly. Start by comforting him and if he is old enough, tell him what is going to happen. Wash his eyes before placing the drops or ointment, using cottonwool soaked in lukewarm water in which you have dissolved a little powdered salt, slightly more than a pinch to a cupful, to the point of just being able to taste the salt. Then place his head backwards and gently put the drops in.

If you are using an eye ointment it will need to go inside the lower lid. Again, explain to your child what you are doing. Then gently pull down the lower lid so that it comes away from the eye. Place the ointment gently on the inner surface and then close the eye. Tell your child to keep it closed for at least half a minute.

For nose drops if your child is old enough, encourage him to blow his nose first. Then, with his head tilted backwards, put the drops into each nostril individually and ask him to take a deep breath through his nose.

Eardrops are put in directly. No attempt should be made to clear the ears out first, as there is a danger that you might force any wax in further, possibly infecting the ear or even damaging the ear drum.

## Skin creams

Local treatment to the skin varies according to the type of disorder. Some creams need to be put on after a bath and some need to be covered by a dressing to prevent the treatment being rubbed off or the skin irritated. Ask your doctor or chemist if you are not sure.

**Eye drops**

Wash the eyes with cottonwool soaked in slightly salted water (see page 122).

Tilt your child's head back and gently put the eye drops in.

**Eye ointments**

After washing the eye, gently place the ointment inside the lower lid.

Tell your child to close his eyes, so that the medicine will spread.

**Nose drops**

Tilt the head, put in the drops and tell your child to breathe in.

**Ear drops**

With your child's head to one side, put the ear drops in directly.

# 3. The right food and drink

In most circumstances no special diet is necessary when a child is ill. There are obvious exceptions, such as diabetes, when sugar should be avoided. Parents should recognize that when they themselves are unwell, they may completely lose their appetite. Why should the child be any different? Force feeding is to be discouraged as this will only cause the child to associate food with bad rather than good events. He should, however, be encouraged to drink and to eat those things which he feels like. Having plenty to drink is important as dehydration can come on slowly or even quite rapidly, especially in the presence of diarrhoea and vomiting. Severe dehydration is potentially quite dangerous, see page 43.

Do not be too distressed by a total loss of appetite even if your child loses weight. He will quickly regain any lost weight and his full appetite on recovery. While the child is ill use your commonsense; fluids are more important than solids.

# 4. Pain

Parents are always distressed when a child is in pain. The feeling of parental impotence is often acute and frustrating. Simple remedies, such as the use of paracetamol or aspirin are often effective and only rarely will it be necessary to use stronger medication. Your doctor will prescribe this. Simple relief may be obtained by giving your child a hot water bottle to place on the sore spot or by gently massaging the area. Most children will tell their parents what makes them feel better.

# 5. Quarantine

The question of whether it is necessary to isolate a sick child from outside friends or from family is often asked. As regards family, there is usually no point in isolation as family members will have been in contact with the disease during its infectious stage before there were any outward signs (such as a rash) by which the disease could be recognized. Simple hygiene measures, such as careful washing of hands and of soiled and potentially infected bedclothes are all that is required. When a child is ill the bedclothes should be changed regularly, possibly as often as two or three times in a week. It may, however, be necessary for members of the family to receive some form of preventive treatment both in order to protect themselves and also to protect other people whom they might meet in their day-to-day lives; examples of this include antibiotics if the child has meningitis or gamma-globulin injections in the case of hepatitis. As regards isolation from friends and school, consult the following table. The diseases themselves are described in the A to Z section in part one.

| Disease | Incubation period* | Infectious period/isolation |
| --- | --- | --- |
| **Chicken pox** | 1–3 weeks | The patient should be isolated until all the spots have crusted. The disease is infectious from 2 days before the outbreak of rash, until all the spots have crusted. |

*Incubation means the time period from exposure to the disease during which the infection is brewing, and before it actually is apparent.

| Disease | Incubation period* | Infectious period/isolation |
|---------|-------------------|----------------------------|
| **German measles (Rubella)** | 2–3 weeks | Isolate until the rash disappears. The patient is infectious from 7 days before the onset of the rash until 5 days or so afterwards. Advise pregnant friends if your child has been in contact with them during the infectious period. They may need medical advice (see page 51). |
| **Glandular fever** | 2–8 weeks | Care should be taken to avoid contact with saliva, for example, avoid sharing cups and toothbrushes, etc., for a period of up to three months. |
| **Infectious hepatitis** | 2–5 weeks | For a minimum of 7 days after onset of jaundice. |
| **Ordinary measles** | 1–2 weeks | Isolate for 5 days after the rash appears. The child in fact was infectious during the stage of catarrh, 10 or so days before the onset of the rash. |
| **Mumps** | 2–4 weeks | Isolate until 7 days after the swelling has begun to subside. Mumps is communicable for 9 days before the swelling of the face began. |
| **Whooping cough (Pertussis)** | Incubation is prolonged; 1–2 weeks of catarrh and another 1–2 weeks until the cough appears. | The patient is in fact infectious in the catarrhal stage but should be isolated and kept off school for 4 weeks after the onset of the cough. The cough itself may be present for 3 months or more. |

*Incubation means the time period from exposure to the disease during which the infection is brewing, and before it actually is apparent.

| Disease | Incubation period* | Infectious period/isolation |
|---------|-------------------|----------------------------|
| **Meningitis** | Depends on the type of meningitis but usually is for a period of about 1–2 weeks. | Until recovered. |
| **Gastroenteritis** | Variable, but may be as short as 24 hours. | Isolate from other children but particularly small infants, until vomiting and diarrhoea have ceased. With certain infections (e.g. from salmonella or shigella bacteria) may be necessary to keep child isolated till it has been demonstrated that the bacteria is not present in stool. |

*Incubation means the time period from exposure to the disease during which the infection is brewing, and before it actually is apparent.

# The child in hospital

Your child may need to be admitted to a hospital because of an emergency, either medical or surgical, or alternatively in order to have certain tests and investigations so that your doctor may arrive at a diagnosis. Most children are now admitted to a children's hospital or alternatively to a paediatric unit in a district general hospital. Try to avoid having your child admitted to an adult ward as it will not have proper provisions for children, whereas children's hospitals and wards are specifically geared to the needs of children.

It is important to minimize any emotional trauma that may result from hospital admission. The child's reaction will vary with his age, his general feeling of security, the state of the parent/child relationship at home, any psychological preparation which has been possible and also the general atmosphere of the ward. Most children can adapt to the environmental change but the

*Children's wards are all geared up to cater for young patients. Parents are welcome to stay with the child as long as possible.*

hospital is a foreign and potentially frightening place and can be upsetting and traumatic for the child, especially as his illness is probably making him low-spirited anyway. Often children have fantasies about what will happen to them and what to expect and this will intermingle with reality. They may have fears of being eaten up by goblins and then see doctors and staff as a real threat. Parents must never use a doctor, nurse or hospital as a threat to children for bad behaviour or threaten to exchange the child when he is naughty. Should a hospital admission be required at any time, threats such as these will inevitably come home to roost.

Children's wards have special provisions for different age groups. There is often a playleader to help keep the children occupied and amused, a teacher to help with schooling, so that time is not lost and nurses and doctors especially trained to anticipate the needs of children and their families. Hospital admission procedures vary from hospital to hospital as does the actual time of admission which is often arranged to fit in with ward procedure. If the admission has been planned in advance then often a pre-admission visit is suggested in order to prepare the child.

Usually on arrival, you are asked for general information about the family, then various routine tests are carried out, for example your child's temperature will be taken as well as his pulse and blood pressure. The doctor may also want a specimen of urine and to take a blood sample. The parents should help the child settle in and advise the staff of particular likes and dislikes. It may help if you take in a favourite toy and certainly any comfort rags or blankets must go too, so that your child does not feel cut off from his own world. If possible, the mother should stay day and night with the child. Most good paediatric units have facilities for mothers to stay and now also encourage visiting by brothers and sisters and other members of the family. Should there be any special precautions, such as quarantine, then the family will be told about these by the staff. It is also best if your child can wear his own clothes but some hospitals do insist that hospital issue is worn. This is in order to limit laundry problems. For the emergency admission, favourite toys, etc., should be brought in as soon as possible.

Sometimes the admission will be merely for a day for special tests or a minor operative procedure. This allows the child to recover at home in his own bed and limits the time taken off from school.

Procedures in hospital can be frightening and distressing, often more for the parent than the child. The child's sense of anxiety, however, can be heightened by transfer from the parent. It is debatable whether or not it is wise for the mother to stay with her infant during procedures such as the taking of blood or the setting up of intravenous infusions. If you feel that such procedures will worry you, you may well transmit your anxiety and make not only your child, but often the doctor, too, nervous. It does not help the medical staff if you faint! It may be better for you not to be present if you feel that you will be upset or cannot control your emotions; on the other hand if you can stay, you may be of considerable help.

A parent should not find a children's ward threatening. The staff will answer questions as truthfully as possible when asked. It is important for you to be fully informed about what is happening to your child. It must be remembered that the parents, together with the medical staff, bear the legal and moral responsibility for the care of the child. Should the family be concerned that care is inadequate, then they should take this up with the doctors concerned.

If you do not understand the reason, nature and implication of tests you should ask. Blood tests check on either the chemical content of the blood or the adequacy of blood constituents. Other tests often depend on specific technology which allows internal visualization of structures – these include different forms of X-ray tests and minor operative procedures, such as the use of endoscopes to look at gut lining and so on.

# After a stay in hospital

Once your child has been discharged from hospital it is as well to be prepared for new behaviour problems. These result from patterns of behaviour picked up in hospital from other children and from the fact that the child is often indulged while ill and has learned a new way of manipulating his parents, or even as a result of fear. He is often subdued, may start continually doing the opposite of what you want or may show evidence of developmental regression. He may begin to have night terrors, start wetting his bed and become more clinging. This is usually a passing phase, which you need to manage very quietly but firmly. The more fuss you make the longer the problem will persist. If, for example, the bed is wet, try to be quite matter-of-fact about it. Change the sheets and say "It happens, don't worry about it", and then carry on gritting your teeth.

In some cases you may need to continue with a specific therapy at home. Ask both the hospital and your own doctor for special advice as to what is required, what is to be expected and how to handle any problems which may arise. Your G.P. should be kept informed by the hospital.

# Difficult circumstances

Parents often feel guilty when their child is ill, especially when other normal pressures prevent them from always being around. Readjustment of daily activities is not always possible but every effort should be made to give the child as much familiar company as possible. Illness is not the parents' fault. Both family and child need to learn to take it in their stride.

If your child is missing too much schooling while at home, ask for advice from your general practitioner, or from the school itself. If he's in hospital, ask the hospital teacher. Arrangements can often be made to provide extra homework and tuition.

If the travel costs of hospital visiting are an extra burden on your budget, financial help is often available through social services. No parents should feel that they cannot afford to visit their child, even if he has been sent to a specialist hospital some distance away.

# PART THREE
# PREVENTION

# Looking after your child's health

The general health of the community in the United Kingdom has improved over the last century. This is due to a better standard of living brought about by higher wages, a better diet, the availability of antibiotics, the decrease in infectious diseases, better housing and social support. The purpose of health care is to provide for the social, mental, emotional and physical needs of the individual.

Health care has two goals. Firstly, prevention which aims to improve the general wellbeing of the individual both in the short and long term and, secondly, crisis intervention where help is given in the event of acute illness. Crisis intervention lies in the province of the family practitioner and the hospital medical services. Prevention, on the other hand, is organized by the doctor, local health clinic, school medical services and social service agencies.

Prevention of childhood illnesses begins, in fact, before conception, and continues through pregnancy and childbirth. The mother-to-be is given information about what is an adequate diet, she is advised to stop smoking, not to take drugs and to try to avoid infectious diseases. Antenatal care is intended to identify a high-risk pregnancy, where there is a possibility of a less than satisfactory outcome, while the obstetrician aims to deliver a healthy child who is able to adapt to, and thrive in the outside world. Several tests aimed at either prevention of illness or early detection of problems are carried out in the immediate newborn period. The infant is examined in order to confirm normality and identify any congenital condition which requires treatment. The baby is given a biochemical screening by the Guthrie test to exclude the rare abnormality of protein chemistry known as Phenylketonuria, which, if left untreated, will cause brain damage. A test is now also carried out to determine whether thyroid function is normal.

In the first year of life advice is available both from the health visitor and the local health clinic. The health visitor is a specially trained nurse, whose role is to identify health and social problems and to provide advice and direction.

Advice is often sought because of feeding difficulties, behaviour and development problems, about home safety, immunization and minor ailments. The infant should be routinely checked in his first six months to see that he has no squint, that his testicles have descended, that his hips are normal and that he can see and hear. It is important if there is a physical or mental handicap that it be diagnosed early, so that remedial measures can be started. There is evidence that early intervention improves the long term outlook.

The Health Service also provides a number of other support services, which include social services and aids for the unemployed, single parent families, sick or disabled parents and children. Financial support through grants (such as the attendance allowance) designed to offset the cost of looking after handicapped children, aiding transport, etc., is available in needy cases. No child need suffer because of his family's financial or social circumstances. Advice on these matters can be obtained from your local or hospital social services department. Often other special circumstances have to be taken into consideration; for example, in certain population groups children may be at risk of rickets because of the traditional diet normally eaten in their households, and so advice is offered to them about vitamin supplements.

# Routine examinations by doctors

There are no set rules as to how often a doctor should see a child for routine assessment. This is left to the good judgement of the parents. Children are seen at least three times in their first year, however, because of the need for vaccinations. Ideally, a child should be seen at birth in order to diagnose any congenital defects (see page 32) and then at two to three months for the first vaccination (see page 144) and again at six months and nine months for the other two.

During these visits it is also convenient to check up on other things, so that the development of vision and hearing can be assessed, common problems dealt with and general progress monitored. At eighteen months to two years the child is again seen at the time of his measles vaccination. His speech and language can be assessed at this time. He will be seen at five years of age on school entry by the school doctor. If there should be anything amiss at any of these examinations, then specialist advice can be sought and any tests needed arranged.

# Well baby clinics

Children are seen in these clinics in the first year of life. The clinics are staffed by trained nurses, health visitors and doctors. The purpose of the visits is to assess the growth and development of your child, and to pick up any deviation from normal early on. In early infancy your child will be weighed without clothes at each visit. A child's weight at this stage is representative of, but not equal to, growth and often too much is made of weight, so that failure to gain weight is a common cause of anxiety in mothers. The important thing is that the infant continues to thrive physically and emotionally.

The causes for being under-weight include not eating enough (which is probably the most common cause), some disturbance of absorption and utilization of food stuffs, chronic illness, vomiting and diarrhoea, infection, especially urinary tract infection, and, more rarely, metabolic and hormone diseases and heart defects. The last three have other tell-tale signs and your doctor and health visitor will be attuned to them.

At the same time as weight is assessed, the baby's length and height will be measured. Usually the naked baby is placed on a measuring board, his legs will be straightened out and the reading taken. At two years of age standing height is measured. Should the length of the infant be way below normal (this is statistically only likely in less than 3 per cent of children) and there is other evidence of the infant failing to thrive, then it may be necessary to seek a cause. The commonest reason for the

*A baby's weight is often used as a guide to his growth and general health. Sick babies do not gain weight but often healthy ones do not either. Weight gain is a guide and not a be-all and end-all. If your baby does not gain weight as expected, your doctor or health visitor will advise you as to the possibilities.*

child to be small is that the parents are short or that the infant was born with a low birth weight. It is, however, possible that some form of malnutrition is the cause or much more rarely serious disorders, such as chromosome abnormalities, chronic illness or congenital heart disease. The baby's head circumference may also be measured to see whether it is bigger or smaller than the norm. As there are problems associated with the head being too big or too small, the doctor may want to do further investigations but most likely the head is the size and shape it is because of hereditary factors.

# Vision testing

Babies can see from birth but have a limited ability to focus. They turn to light and will look at faces. Adult vision is achieved by six months. It is important to diagnose a vision problem early because children need normal sight in order to learn depth and spatial perception and achieve co-ordination. The most common disorder is one of a squint (see page 90). A squint is common up to four months of age. Should the squint persist to six months of age, see your doctor about it, so that corrective measures can be taken if necessary.

# Hearing tests

Normal hearing is necessary in order to develop language. Hearing may be abnormal because of a hereditary cause, where there is a family history of hearing loss, or because of damage in the first few days of life caused by an abnormally high level of jaundice or persistent viral infection. Hearing can be assessed from as early as six to nine months of age. This is done at the Health Clinic, where the nurse will find out whether the child can hear certain sounds. If there is any room for doubt, your child will be referred to a specialist who will perform more specific hearing tests.

If, in his normal daily life, your child does not react to sound or if you notice that he has stopped his usual babbling, then it is worth checking up with your doctor. Hearing can also be defective in children who have recurrent middle ear infections (see page 66). When necessary, hearing aids can be applied or surgery performed at a very early age. The long-term outcome can be improved by early detection and intervention. In older children hearing loss can occur due to repeated and chronic ear infections so it is important to test hearing after such an illness.

# Language testing

It is important to have a child assessed who has no understandable speech by two years of age and certainly if the mother cannot understand his speech by 2½ years of age. However, it is not unusual that a stranger cannot fully understand a child's speech until the age of four.

Problems in speech include articulation problems, for example, Th sounds are pronounced as F and Rs as Ws and so on. These usually correct themselves. Stammering is also common and provided little fuss is made it generally improves with increasing age.

Speech problems have a number of causes. They may be due to shyness, to emotional or psychological problems, to lack of stimulation, to mental retardation, to problems with articulation and to some hearing problems. The most common cause is, in fact, a hearing loss.

# Developmental assessment

Rapid changes in growth and development occur throughout infancy and early childhood. The pace of development is usually genetically determined, although the child's environment is also important. If the child is given lots of attention and different distractions, then learning new things will become a matter of course. If left entirely to his own devices, however, he may make little or no progress. Your doctor or health visitor will keep a general eye on your child's development. They will be assessing changes in development, particularly at times when

## Warning signs indicating potential developmental problems

| | |
|---|---|
| **Six weeks** | Excess floppiness of the head. |
| | Differences in tone (feel) or movements between the four limbs. |
| **Three months** | No social responses (e.g. smile, recognition). |
| | No response to sound. |
| **Six months** | Persistent fisting of the hands. |
| | Persistent differences in tone (feel), reflexes and movement between the four limbs. |
| | Abnormal reflexes. |
| | Persistent squint. |
| **Nine–Twelve months** | Unable to sit up by self. |
| | Unable to bear weight on legs. |
| | No babbling noises. |
| | Abnormal movements. |
| | Abnormal reflexes. |
| **Eighteen months** | No spontaneous speech. |
| | No standing. |
| | No pincer grasp by hand. |
| **Twenty-four months** | No walking. |
| | No words with meaning. |
| **Thirty-six months** | Speech unintelligible. |

statistically your child is most vulnerable and failure to progress may indicate a deeper problem. So, in general, the assessment is carried out through informal observations, but should any of the warning signs listed in the table on page 139, or no evident developmental progress, be noted, then your child may be seen by a specialist for a more formal assessment. As a general rule, early intervention in some developmental problem will reduce the long term effects.

It is common for mothers to compare their infants, especially as to who is doing what and when and how well and then ask the question "why isn't mine?". These sorts of comparisons provoke fruitless anxiety. Wide ranges of normal exist. Some children walk at one year and others not till they are 18 months old – both are normal, both children will be equally good footballers all else being equal. If you are genuinely worried seek advice.

# School medical

This examination is usually carried out shortly after your child begins school. It is performed by a school doctor or nurse. Should your child be going to a private school it may be necessary for you to arrange this examination through your family doctor. The aim of the examination is to diagnose any physical, visual, hearing, language, or behavioural problem which will limit the child's ability to compete in school and learn normally. It is also intended to help assess common medical problems which may interfere with the ability to participate in school activities. An example of this is the child who has significant asthma, where special allowance may need to be made during PE classes or with sports.

# Visits to the dentist

Regular care of both milk and permanent teeth is important. The first deciduous (or milk) tooth will appear at around five to seven months and the rest follow during the next two and a half years. A child will grow twenty milk teeth in all. The first to erupt are usually the lower incisors. These are the sharp chisel-like teeth at the front used for cutting. The last teeth to appear are the second molars, which are the square teeth at the back of the mouth, used for grinding. You should take care of these early teeth or you can run the risk of damage to the structure, association and shape of the second, permanent set.

Daily tooth brushing with a soft brush should begin from the moment the first teeth appear and regular dental check-ups should begin from around three years. It is a good idea to use a fluoride-containing toothpaste, and in fact almost all tooth-pastes on the market will have this ingredient. Fluoride makes the enamel (the outer protective covering of the teeth) resistant to decay. In areas where the water supply is not fluoridated, or has a low fluoride content, fluoride supplements should be given. This can be given in the form of drops for young children or tablets for older ones and the amount varies according to the amount of fluoride in your water supply. Your local water authority will tell you what the figure is and your dentist will advise you about the need for supplements.

Some nutritional deficiencies and diseases can delay the eruption of teeth, so if you are concerned, see your doctor. It is not uncommon, however, for the first tooth not to appear before the first birthday.

The second set of teeth (permanent teeth) begin to erupt at five to six years, as the deciduous teeth are shed. Eruption continues until twelve years of age (except the wisdom teeth). With certain rare diseases teeth may fall out at other times.

There are three aspects involved in looking after your child's teeth: brushing, diet and visits to the dentist. Firstly, teeth should be cleaned regularly after meals and at night. Up to three years of age, you will have to do it for your child but after that you should only have to supervise. Only use a small amount of toothpaste (about the size of a small pea) and a soft brush. Brush up and down over all the teeth and gums. If you have difficulty doing it properly with an ordinary toothbrush, try an electric

It is important to have a regular routine for looking after teeth. Daily brushing of teeth with a fluoride-containing toothpaste and providing a good diet, along with visits to the dentist, are the best guardians of children's teeth.

one. These introduce the element of fun into tooth brushing and, when used properly, do a good job.

Secondly, a healthy diet is important. Once your child is weaned, give some raw, crunchy foods every so often and try to avoid too many sweets, cakes or soft drinks, particularly last thing at night. Never use a dummy (pacifier) which has been dipped in honey or jam. You are also not doing your child any favours by allowing him to go to sleep sucking a bottle with sweetened juice. The sugar is fermented by bacteria in the mouth and this causes a breakdown of the tooth enamel and decay. You should not bribe your children with sweets; ration them as treats, rather than forbidding them altogether.

Thirdly, regular visits should be made to the dentist, once your child is three years old. The dentist will probably recommend routine check-ups every six months.

# Immunization

Immunization or vaccination are terms used to describe the injection of a particular bacteriological organism into the body which will artificially produce an internal protection against certain diseases. The vaccine comprises either a killed or a partially inactive organism of the disease itself. It works by stimulating the body to react against it in a way that it would for the actual disease, so that when the real infection comes along, the body remembers how to react and sets up defences, thus preventing the disease from taking hold. In this way illnesses such as diphtheria and smallpox, which at one time were major killers, are now largely eradicated. Also as the number of protected people in the community increases, the chance of a

*All children should receive a course of injections from their general practitioner as immunization against infectious diseases. This is good for the child and for the community. The introduction of immunization programmes has helped eradicate many of the killer diseases.*

particular disease taking hold in epidemiç proportions is reduced. The common vaccines available are against diphtheria, tetanus, whooping cough, polio, measles, mumps, German measles and tuberculosis. New experimental vaccines are being developed against some of the common bacterial infections, which cause, for example, meningitis.

Vaccines containing already formed antibodies can also be used in some circumstances. These are known as gamma-globulin injections. The most commonly used one protects against hepatitis but you can also protect against chicken pox and other viral illnesses if necessary.

Various schedules for immunization have been recommended, for example, triple vaccine (diphtheria, tetanus and whooping cough (pertussis), plus polio) is given in some areas at three months, six months and nine months, whereas in other areas it is given at two, four and six months. Each schedule is effective: what is important is that three doses are given in the first year of life and that with live vaccines, such as polio vaccine, there is a six week to two month gap between doses.

If one of the course of injections has been missed for some reason it is only necessary to give the missed injection and not restart the whole course.

A suggested outline for immunization is given below.

| | |
|---|---|
| *Three months:* | Diphtheria/tetanus/pertussis/plus polio |
| *Six months:* | Diphtheria/tetanus/pertussis/plus polio |
| *Nine months:* | Diphtheria/tetanus/pertussis/plus polio |
| *Fifteen to eighteen months:* | Measles (plus or minus mumps/rubella) |
| *Five years:* | Diphtheria/tetanus/plus polio |
| *Adolescence:* | Rubella to girls who have not previously had the illness, or the earlier injection. B.C.G. vaccine against tuberculosis. |

Early immunization in the first year of life is aimed primarily at preventing whooping cough. This is a serious disease in the first six months of life and the infant is not protected by antibodies which cross the placenta from the mother. The infection is generally introduced into the home by school-age children. The use of whooping cough vaccine is currently controversial (see below), although the general thinking of paediatricians and current recommendation of the Department of Health is to include it in the schedule. The incidence and severity of the disease is at the moment far worse than the risk associated with the vaccine.

Routine immunization should be postponed if your child is ill and has a high temperature; it is alright to continue if your child merely has a common cold, but ask your doctor's advice first. Live viral vaccines such as measles, mumps and polio should not be given to children who are taking steroid drugs or who have a medically known immune system defect.

## Pertussis (whooping cough)

There has been much publicity recently about the risk of vaccine damage and resulting mental and physical retardation from the whooping cough vaccine. The severe complication rate is roughly 1 in 1-300,000 vaccinations. Because this publicity has persuaded parents over the last few years not to allow their children to be vaccinated, there are currently more children being admitted to hospital with whooping cough and there is a far greater death rate and complication rate from the disease proper than from vaccine damage. Current recommendations are to include the vaccine in the schedule. It should, however, not be given in the following circumstances:

(a) Where there is a history of convulsions in immediate family members, or if there have been convulsions or any evidence of brain irritation, such as due to low blood sugar, infection or low oxygen, in the newborn period.
(b) Where there is evidence of marked developmental delay.
(c) After three years of age.
(d) If there has been a severe local or a general reaction to an earlier dose.

It is generally safe to give the vaccine to infants who were pre-term. Your doctor will advise you.

After vaccination, it is not uncommon for your child to have an area of redness around the point of the injection and for his arm to be painful. Persistent screaming, however, may mean a serious reaction. If your child develops this, call your doctor straightaway.

## Diphtheria

This vaccine is generally not given to children after ten years of age, unless they have had a prior test (Schick Test) to detect the risk of reaction. The reactions to the diphtheria component in the vaccine include possible swelling in the area of the injection, a hard nodule may be noticed and a slight fever. The swelling settles over one to two days; the nodule may persist for longer.

## Polio

Polio vaccination occasionally results in mild, shortlived diarrhoea. Treatment is rarely necessary.

## Measles

The measles vaccine is a live viral vaccine. It should not be given till 15–18 months of age, as immunity does not develop in the period after the birth, because of competition from antibodies originally passed through the mother's placenta and persisting in the child's bloodstream. Vaccination should also not be carried out in infants who have a history of allergy, a history of convulsions, active tuberculosis or who have a defect in their immune system. After vaccination there may be a mild reaction in the form of a fever or a rash. In North America this vaccine is commonly given in combination with rubella and mumps vaccines but is rarer in the U.K.

## Rubella (German measles)

In North America it is common to immunize both boys and girls in the second year of life. Current recommendations in the United Kingdom are that this vaccine should only be given to teenage girls who have not previously had the illness and before the first pregnancy. This is because if a woman catches the disease in the first three months of her pregnancy, there is a high risk of damage to the unborn child. Several days of mild joint pains are common after this injection.

## B.C.G.

This vaccine is used to protect against tuberculosis. It is given to close family contacts (including babies) of people who have the disease or are at special risk, such as nurses. It should not be given to children with eczema or other skin disorders. It is however commonly given to teenagers at school who have been tested to see whether they have previously been exposed to tuberculosis. The use of the vaccine in this way is aimed at eradicating this disease. Vaccination programmes at school vary from area to area.

Reactions to immunization are not uncommon. The parent should be prepared for the child to have a slight temperature, which may in fact rise sufficiently to cause a febrile convulsion (see page 35). The child may also be irritable and there may be redness and swelling on the site of the injection. Paracetamol or junior aspirin can be given to limit these reactions; some doctors recommend that you do this routinely.

Serious reactions are rare. Persistent screaming is a worrying sign. If you are concerned you should consult your doctor immediately.

# Nutrition

There are five basic nutrients – proteins, carbohydrates, fats, minerals and vitamins. A balance of all five is necessary for a healthy diet. The calorie content (this is a measure of energy value of food) of the diet is also important. The calorie needs of a child will vary according to his age, height, weight and physical activity. When calculating the food requirements of a child it is not just the day-to-day activity which should be taken into account but also the need for reserves for growth. Surplus calories are converted to fat for future use.

Proteins are complex chemicals made up of subunits known

as aminoacids. They are important for growth and tissue repair and regeneration. Proteins are found in animal products such as meat, fish, eggs and milk and also in vegetables and grains.

Carbohydrates, or sugars, are the main immediate source of energy for the body. Carbohydrates are present in sweet foods and in vegetables such as potatoes.

Fats, found in, for example, butter, nuts, meat and milk, provide the long term source of energy.

Minerals are important for the development of healthy bones and teeth (for example, calcium) and for the formation of red blood cells (for example, iron). Other minerals are important for normal function of different tissues, an example here is iodine which is required for the thyroid gland to work properly.

Vitamins are substances which the body does not make and which, therefore, need to be provided by the diet. A letter is commonly used to describe the vitamin, for example, Vitamin D. Vitamins provide essential link chemicals to enable the body's metabolism to work properly. If there is a deficiency, disease often results, for example, if there is a long term deficiency in the diet of Vitamin D, then rickets will result.

The make-up of a child's diet is described below, according to his age.

## Feeding from 0–4 months

**Breast feeding** During the first four months of life, milk from either breast or bottle will be a child's only food. The composition of breast milk will vary from mother to mother and from day to day but, on balance, provided the mother's diet is adequate, breast milk will supply all the nutritional demands of the young infant required for growth and energy expenditure.

The advantages of breast feeding as opposed to bottle feeding include a lower incidence of the following disorders:
- Gastroenteritis
- Ear infections
- Upper respiratory tract infections and chest infections
- Milk allergies
- Other allergies such as asthma and eczema
- Overfeeding and errors in making up the feed
- Sudden infant death syndrome (cot death)

Emotional advantages to both mother and infant also exist

with breast feeding. Many of the above advantages, particularly the lower incidence of allergies, can be lost by giving even *one* artificial feed early on.

The mother's milk supply is dependent, to a large extent, on the frequency of the feeding. It is not possible to overfeed a breast fed baby. Frequently the mother is concerned that her baby is not getting enough milk. Test weighing the baby before and after a feed will give an idea of the individual feed's volume. Test-weighing, however, frequently promotes anxiety rather than allaying it and is probably best avoided. The important thing is whether the baby is contented, thriving and steadily gaining weight. The main causes of insufficient milk supply are when the mother is not eating enough of the right foods (she needs approximately 500–1000 extra calories per day), or when the baby is not properly latched on to the breast or allowed to feed for a long enough period. There may be problems in sucking when the baby has a local infection in the mouth, such as thrush, or is tired from having been allowed to cry too long. The mother need not be concerned that breast feeding will spoil the shape of her breasts.

**Bottle/Formula feeding** Proprietary formula milks have been developed to be similar in chemical composition to breast milk. The milks have all been fortified with vitamins and minerals, and there is very little to choose between the different brands. It is common practice to change milks if a child should continually vomit or be difficult with feeding – it probably makes very little difference as to which brand is chosen but the change does make the mother feel better and seems occasionally to be of benefit. The aim of formula feeding is also to provide adequate calories and fluids for growth and activity, the volume chosen is based on the weight and age of the child.

The major advantage of formula feeding is convenience in that it gives the mother independence by allowing someone else, such as the father, to feed the baby. One does avoid the minor risk of drug transference in milk from the mother and the actual intake of the infant can be calculated. All the immunological advantages of breast milk are, however, lost. There are also risks, namely overfeeding the infant, which can cause later obesity; the fat content of the milk may predispose the infant to heart disease as an adult; if the feeds are not hygienically prepared, there is the risk of infection; or if too much powder is added, the baby takes in an extra biochemical load, which his body cannot handle.

With certain diseases special formulations are available, for example a soy formula may be recommended if the child is allergic to cow's milk protein. There are also special formulas for children with metabolic disorders, such as phenylketonuria, galactosaemia, and sugar intolerance.

It is important that the feed is properly prepared as per the instructions on the package. Water should be pre-boiled before the formula is added. It is a mistake to boil the formula once it is reconstituted as this will cause it to be over concentrated. Most parents warm the feed but this is largely a question of taste. It probably makes very little difference to the baby if the formula is offered cold. It should, however, not be either boiling or refrigerator cold.

**Vitamin and iron supplements** There is still some controversy as to whether there is a need for extra vitamin and iron supplements in infancy. Proprietary formulas are already fortified and in mothers on a good diet, breast milk should be

*Breast feeding is satisfying to both mother and baby; there is a special closeness between them, no complicated preparation is necessary and the milk is always served at the right temperature. A lower incidence of infections and allergies and a good nutritional balance are other factors which make breast feeding the ideal form of infant feeding.*

adequate. In certain population groups, however, it is recommended that extra Vitamin D is given. This is in order to prevent rickets and to help with the formation of strong bones. There are no universal guidelines as to the use of vitamin supplements; the recommendations vary from doctor to doctor and clinic to clinic. Extra vitamins (the common ones are A, C, D drops and tablets) do no harm provided they are not taken to excess. Instructions as to dosage must be carefully followed. Pre-term babies will probably receive vitamins (particularly D) from about one month till at least the end of the first year.

By six months of age the baby will have exhausted his iron stores which were built up when he was in the womb and, unless a solid diet including green vegetables and eggs has been introduced by then, iron supplements are necessary, in order to prevent anaemia. Both cow's milk and human milk are variously deficient in iron; pre-term infants who missed out on getting their full quota of iron and babies whose mothers had a relatively poor diet, should probably receive iron supplements from one month of age. These will usually be prescribed by your doctor or health clinic. The question of fluoride supplements is mentioned on page 141.

*For some families, bottle feeding is the only way. It allows the father to participate in what is an important activity in the baby's early life; it frees the mother from an otherwise tight schedule, so that she can relax or go out while someone else takes on the task. A whole generation has been successfully reared on artificial formula.*

## Common problems

There are various common problems associated with the milk diet in the first four months and these are described below. Advice on problems in feeding can be obtained from your health visitor, local health clinic, family practitioner or paediatrician.

**(a) Failure to establish a feeding pattern.** Many mothers are upset when their newborn baby does not stick to a timed pattern of feeding. This is especially so when they have had their baby in hospital, where the nursing staff often (unfortunately) attempt to keep to a rigid four-hourly routine. The truth is that each of us is hungry at different times and if it should not be a meal-time, we have a between-meal snack. Babies are the same. Thus an ideal pattern for feeding the newborn is demand feeding, in which the baby is offered milk, either by breast or bottle, when he desires it. With this routine, however, there is a real danger that the bottle-fed baby will be given too much milk. In this case, the mother needs to distinguish between the cry of hunger and that of loneliness.

**(b) Vomiting/possetting.** Small vomits or spitting associated with wind are common after a feed. It is usually due to the milk that lies on top of an air bubble being expelled. Occasionally it is due to the reflux of milk from the stomach into the oesophagus (gullet). If the baby persistently brings up milk and occasionally even large quantities, adding a little milk product, such as plain yogurt, to thicken the feed may help, but ask your doctor's advice first. It might also help if the baby is kept in a semi-sitting position by propping up his cot or nursing him on a pillow or baby chair for a while after the feed to allow the stomach to empty properly. Projectile or forceful vomiting (see page 99) is an important symptom and you should see your doctor about it.

**(c) Wind.** Both the bottle and breast-fed baby swallow air during feeding. Should the baby be an air swallower, then it is important to wind him mid-way through the feed. Air swallowing can be recognized in the guzzling breast-fed baby who clearly swallows when not properly latched on, while in the bottle-fed baby if the air-milk layer in the bottle is below the teat, air will be swallowed and lots of air bubbles will be seen in the bottle. If the baby is not winded, he may vomit small amounts of milk or alternatively appear not to be hungry and then when the wind is passed, will wake up wanting more food.

**(d) Colic.** Colic appears at about two weeks of age and disappears mysteriously around three months. The baby seems in genuine pain, his abdomen is tense and he draws his legs up. It is usually worse at night (oh why?) or seems to be; the infant will not settle and screams continuously. There may be several attacks per day. It occurs in both bottle and breast-fed babies. In the breast-fed infant several causes have been suggested; it may be related to the mother's intake of cow's milk or due to foods and spices which cross through the breast milk and which disagree with the baby. In bottle-fed babies it is thought to be due to one of the milk proteins.

Treatment is difficult and the only thing that truly provides relief is the passage of wind.

You can try walking around with the baby firmly draped over your shoulder; gentle pressure on the abdomen seems to help.

Gripe water helps in some cases and antispasmodic drugs from your doctor can be tried.

It usually goes at three months of age much to everyone's (including the doctor's) relief.

**(e) Constipation.** This, in a small baby, is generally due to underfeeding and will settle if you increase the amount of fluids (see also page 34). Occasionally it is necessary to add a little brown sugar to the milk (your clinic will advise you). When you change from breast to bottle, it is normal for the consistency of the stool to change. The previously fluid stool may become progressively firmer in consistency. This does not mean that the infant is constipated and is quite normal. True constipation in the young baby, meaning hard and infrequent stools, occasionally suggests a genuine medical abnormality: hypothyroidism (low thyroid function) and some bowel disorders can occasionally declare themselves in this way. Your doctor will be able to tell you if it is abnormal.

**(f) Diarrhoea.** By this the doctor means frequent fluid stools (see also page 43). The cause may be either an infection or if the child cannot cope with some type of food, usually a sugar or fat. By avoiding the offending food for a time, the condition will usually improve. The problem with frequent and excessive diarrhoea is that the baby may become dehydrated. This requires treatment.

**(g) Failure to gain weight.** Parents often place more emphasis on this than does the doctor or clinic. Provided that the infant is in every other way thriving, a failure to gain weight over a matter of days or weeks is often of no significance. Persistent failure to gain weight, however, might be of concern. What is of more concern is if the infant actually loses weight. The infant's weight can be plotted against his age on charts and then allowances made for expected deviations from the norm. Should the infant be grossly under-weight and failing to thrive, he should be given a thorough check-up to make sure he is not suffering from serious disease. A hospital assessment may be necessary.

**(h) Over feeding/obesity.** Over feeding occurs only in the bottle-fed infant. The breast-fed infant is able to regulate his own intake, whereas the parent regulates the intake of the bottle-fed baby. The seeds of later obesity are laid in this period (see also page 72). Remember that a bottle is not a universal solution to crying, sometimes a cuddle is all that's needed.

**(i) Time taken to feed.** At most, a feed, either breast or bottle, should take no more than twenty minutes. If longer is required in the bottle-fed baby, you should check to see whether the teat hole is the right size. Breast-fed babies often wish to suck longer. This is usually for emotional comfort rather than because of an inadequate supply.

**(j) Hiccups.** These are not uncommon in babies. Hiccups cause no harm and usually settle after a few minutes.

# Four to six months

The age at which solids are introduced into the diet (termed mixed feeding or weaning) is a common cause of concern for parents and is in fact controversial. Recommendations vary and over the years the age has been progressively creeping downwards; this is because of the obsession which many parents and doctors have with the concept of adequate weight gain. Those who are doubtful about the early introduction to mixed feeding are worried that it will lay the seeds for later medical problems such as obesity and ischaemic heart disease due to the added carbohydrate, fat, salt and calorie intake. Fat children often become fat adults. There is also a higher statistical risk of infections and allergies in babies who are started on solids too early, particularly, but not only, if at the expense of breast milk. The scientific question as to when the gut enzymes and other systems are sufficiently mature to cope with mixed feeding has also not been answered.

The problem comes about because of the need to plan for the average baby, whereas this animal does not exist. Current recommendations are that solids should not be introduced before four to six months of age. Each new food should be introduced singly. Initially, the food should be of semi-fluid consistency and can be given by a spoon. The amount early on is not important as the nutrition needs of the infant continue to be covered by the milk intake. Tinned foods can be used, or alternatively the mother can blend food she has cooked herself. Neither sugar nor salt should be added, nor should it be seasoned to the mother's own taste. Added salt has no nutritional value and may cause harm (later blood pressure problems), most foods contain enough salt to meet daily needs. There is an almost limitless variety of baby foods on the market; these, however, may bear little relationship to the tastes and textures of food eaten later in life. There is a risk that tinned food designed for the average child may, in fact, impair nutrition in an individual child; on the one hand, in some foods less calories are available per unit volume of food compared with milk and the child gets insufficient food, while on the other, the opposite may be true and a high calorie intake brings with it the risk of obesity. Both types can be filling, it is important that the right balance is struck and this is not always easy, though, in fact, mistakes are rarely made!

The first food to be introduced is usually a fruit (bananas are good!), a cereal or rice. After this has been accepted and enjoyed you can gradually introduce vegetables and other foods, one by one, so that your child eventually becomes used to a variety of colour, flavour and textures. A useful trick is to make individual foods in batches yourself, blend them to the desired texture and then store them in small amounts suitable for one meal in a freezer, as one makes ice for drinks. These can then be taken out and heated up at a later date.

What must be resisted is the question of competition between babies; just because little Johnnie next door, who is the same age, is taking solids, there is no reason why your child should also be on them. Let Johnnie be fat!

## Six months to one year

Through this age period you should progressively introduce foods that are of firmer consistency and require chewing. These include minces, meats and fish. Eating should be the time when the baby learns skills, such as manners and when he can be integrated into family activities. It is safe to introduce doorstep cow's milk from about seven to nine months onwards. In the United States, however, paediatricians recommend that infant formulas continue to be used to about one year of age.

## After one year

By this time the child should be on a variation of a normal adult diet. There should be a balance of protein, carbohydrate, fat, vitamins and minerals. Protein is obtained from milk, meat, fish, vegetable, etc., carbohydrate from cereals and vegetables, and fats from various oils, meat and fish. Minerals and vitamins will also be obtained from these foods. It is not unreasonable, however, to continue any multi-vitamin supplements which you may be giving or to make sure that your child has a daily drink of fresh fruit juice. By one year of age, the child will be eating three times a day with the family. It is not uncommon for the breast-fed baby to occasionally still want to be put to the breast. Breast-feeding ideally should be discontinued only when the baby no longer has the desire for it.

## Later feeding problems

Several of the disorders associated with mixed feeding are due to the intake of either too few or too many nutrients; included are anaemia, retarded growth and stunted development, increased infections and so on, but these are relatively rare. There may be allergies, such as milk intolerance, which lead to diarrhoea, skin rashes and behaviour problems. The most common complaint, however, is one of fad phases and food refusal.

It is common for the toddler at about two years of age to virtually stop eating (at least in the mother's eyes!). He will eat only as much as he needs and often only what he has a taste for. There is a physiological explanation for this. At this stage of development, the rate of growth, and therefore the calorie requirements, normally decrease and with this there is a fall-off in appetite. This often causes great anxiety to the parents who believe their child will starve himself to death. He won't. Parents often have quite unrealistic demands at mealtimes and this creates problems; mealtimes are taken out of the realms of pleasure and into the arena of childhood manipulation. Parents often go to amazing lengths in order to tempt or bribe their children to eat. This is taken advantage of by a clever toddler and a cycle of behaviour problems is set up.

The parents' attitude should be one of calmness but firmness. If your child refuses to eat a particular item or meal do not replace it with an alternative but rather ignore the incident. Think to yourself, however, whether there was a reason, such as was the portion offered far too big; was the child hungry; was he perhaps distracted by other interests, such as a television set in the other room; was he attention-seeking for some reason; was the food unfamiliar; was it a passing dislike or was he just feeling off colour? Whichever one of the reasons you decide was to blame will determine how you approach it next time. You must just use your commonsense, not get angry or upset and not be bullied.

Occasionally a child will require a special diet because of some illness. For example a child with Coeliac disease requires a gluten-free diet, Phenylketonuria requires a phenylalanine-free diet, a low carbohydrate diet will be needed by a diabetic child or a milk-free diet by one who has a milk intolerance. If your child needs one of these diets, you will be advised by your doctor and a dietitian.

'Junk food' should be avoided when possible and certainly should not be allowed to become a mainstay of the daily diet. Junk food frequently has a high carbohydrate content which brings with it the risk of obesity, often has excessive salt leading to later blood pressure and heart problems, or there is a high content of flavour-enhancing or food stabilizing additives. Food additives are thought by several investigators to cause slight neurological problems which lead to behaviour disorders and learning problems. Although these theories have not been totally proven, they equally cannot be totally discounted.

# Clothing and shoes

**Clothing:** In general, a child's clothing should be geared to the activity being undertaken. Clothing should not be to suit parents' or grandparents' ego, but rather be simple, easy to get into and out of and not cause a fuss if it should get dirty. To avoid jealousy, younger children should occasionally receive new clothes in their own right and not just hand-me-downs.

**Shoes:** When children start to walk it is most likely to be indoors, so shoes and socks are not necessary. If the parents insist on a child wearing bootees, etc., care must be taken that there is ample room for growth. Shoes are not needed to give extra support at this stage. Once your child needs outdoor shoes, they should be expertly fitted and it is fit which is important, not the appearance. They should be painless to wear, have ample room for growth, have supple uppers which bend easily in walking and yet provide support. High ankle support is not necessary even with the youngest child. Buckles are often easier to handle than laces.

A common problem in early infancy is flat feet (see also page 47). This is due to the filling out of the fatty pad in the foot. What is important is that the feet are symmetrical and that the joints function normally. If the feet are symmetrical it should be possible to draw an imaginary straight line from the knee to the ground which would pass through the ankle and not inside or outside of it. If the feet do turn in or out (by this test), support shoes may be necessary. Bowing of the knees, and in- or out-turning of the feet are quite normal in a toddler (see also pages 63 and 76). These problems generally correct themselves over two to three years.

# Accidents and safety

Accidents are the single most common cause of death in the one to fourteen year age group. They account for around 30 per cent of deaths in this group and for many hours of the doctors' and hospitals' time. The child is at risk from many accidents both in the home and outside it. Commonsense and vigilance by the parents and child-minders are necessary. One must be careful, however, not to be excessively protective, thereby limiting the child's freedom and taking away all adventurousness.

Children are at risk from all common accidents which befall adults; the motor vehicle accident, drowning, fires, falls, cuts and bruises, suffocation, foreign body inhalation, food inhalation, poisoning and so on. They are also liable to certain accidents because they are not aware of the potential dangers. Parents cannot protect them from unforeseeable disaster, but they can take a number of simple precautions to increase the safety aspects at home and out of doors as detailed below.

# Safety around the home

**Electric plugs** These should all
be covered. Simple covers can
be obtained from department
stores. Children have a
habit of poking fingers
and objects into all sorts
of holes and there is a
real danger of
electrocution.
Remember not to
use electric
blankets with
children who wet
the bed. Unplug
all appliances
when not in
use.

**Fires** These should be kept guarded at all times. There is a
danger of clothes catching alight or children burning themselves. Children should not be left alone in the room with a fire.
Don't let your children play with matches.

**Kitchens** Plastic bags, etc., should be kept out of reach so that a curious child does not put his head inside and suffocate himself. Knives, forks, etc., should also be kept away from toddlers. Children should never be left unattended in the kitchen when there is cooking going on, and saucepan handles should be turned in so that boiling hot food or water cannot easily be pulled down and spilt on the child. Cooker guards can be fitted, so that pans cannot be pulled off the stove. Common cleansers should be kept out of reach.

**Bathroom** Bathroom cleansers should be out of reach, medicines also should be kept in locked cupboards. All medicines should have child-resistant safety caps on the bottle. Young children should not be left unsupervised in the bath: you don't need much water to drown.

**Toys** There are certain features which make some toys unsafe for children, so look out for them before buying toys. All toy material should be non-toxic. There should not be small items, such as plastic eyes, which can be torn off and put in the mouth and swallowed. An infant can cut himself on sharp metal pieces and working mechanisms can trap small fingers.

**Garden shed** Chemicals and paint should be kept out of reach. Do not keep weed killer, etc., in a pop bottle where it can be mistaken for lemonade! Care should be exercised when electric mowers and tools are being used. Make sure that toddlers cannot open garden gates and get out on to the street.

**General** Care must be taken with open windows, especially with those upstairs. Gates should be available for the stairs to prevent toddlers tumbling down or climbing up. Furniture, especially bedroom furniture, should be checked for safety, for example, the space between cot bars should not be such that a young head can get stuck in between.

# Outside the home

Potential danger areas include cars, natural areas a child might care to explore, streams, high walls and playground areas, where there is little room to run around and with a lot of concrete and flying swings. Children, particularly when small, should be supervised as much as possible.

## Road safety

In the United States it is said that the number one preventable cause of death in childhood is accidents associated with cars and road safety: 70,000 children under 5 years of age are injured per year while riding in cars and over 1,000 of those die.

Infants and children should always be restrained in appropriate safety harnesses or child safety seats. They must not be allowed to travel in the front of the car and not be allowed loose in the back. Childproof locks should be fitted to the car doors. It is not safe to travel with a baby held tightly in his mother's arms; even a crash of 30 miles per hour will cause the baby to be ripped out of her arms with a force similar to falling from a three-storey building. Babies can be transported in carrycots, properly enclosed and strapped to the seat, in the rear of the car. When using the car's seat belts only the lap should be used – the sash could dangerously cut a small child in an accident. There is some evidence as well that properly secured children behave better in cars, are less car sick and even are more likely to fall asleep!

Once your child can walk, take care to teach him road traffic rules though young children should not be allowed to cross the road by themselves. Instruction should also be given on road safety to children who are allowed out on bicycles.

# Road Safety: in the car

Babies should never travel in the front of the car and should not be carried in parents' arms. They should be tucked away safe and secure in a carry cot restrained by a proper harness, fixed to the back seat.

The infant who can sit up and the toddler should not be left unrestrained in a car, even for short journeys. They need to be in the back of the car, in a properly fitted, child's car seat with safety belts.

There are also special harnesses for school-aged children, which are fitted to the back seat of a car. Alternatively, an ordinary car seat belt can be worn, but it is advisable to use only the lap portion.

# The green cross code

*The Green Cross code is designed to teach children safety on the roads. All children should learn the code and you can start teaching them the basics from a very early age. To start with, this will be by your example, then gradually you can explain the simple rules, until they become automatic reflexes for the child.*

Find a safe place to cross, with a clear view, not between parked cars.

Stand on the pavement near the kerb, but not on the very edge.

Look first to the right, then left, then to the right again. Listen as well.

Don't try to beat an oncoming car. Let it pass. Look all round again.

When the road is clear, cross quickly but do not run – you may trip.

Keep looking both ways as you cross just in case another car suddenly comes along.

# Cycling Proficiency

*Cycling proficiency lessons teach children how to ride safely. Clothing which can be easily seen should be worn; reflector belts are advisable. Make sure the bike is in proper working order, especially the brakes, the steering and the tyres.*

# Water safety

Water can be dangerous; drowning is a common cause of accidental death, particularly in the adolescent age group. Teach your child to swim as soon as possible! Babies as young as six months old, can be introduced to the pleasures of a swimming pool. Local pools often reserve time for parents with very young children or have pools specially designed for young bathers.

Children should be taught that all water areas can be hazardous and places, such as open drains and ponds, are dangerous. With many water sports, such as boating, life jackets are a wise precaution.

## General

Obviously there are risks to daily life. Due care is, however, necessary. Children often stumble into things quite innocently and are not aware of the dangers. Particular supervision is necessary in playground areas where there are climbing frames, concrete and long falls possible. Commonsense should prevail at all times.

# Hygiene

## Personal hygiene

It is important for parents and children to realise that poor personal hygiene is a common cause of infection and other illnesses. The commonest way for bacteria to be transmitted from one person to another is by what is known as the ano-oral route. One person fails to wash his hands properly after using the toilet and then touches another person. Personal hygiene involves regular washing of person and clothes and careful handwashing after using the toilet and before meals.

Bathing of the child is not only a means of washing off accumulated secretions, the smell of which may become offensive, but it also keeps the skin clear of bacteria. A nappy rash, for example, which is common in small babies, is caused when the skin becomes raw after being left in contact for some time with urine, which forms ammonia which then irritates the skin. The skin may subsequently become infected. Any body area which is allowed to remain moist is a potential cause of infections, so after a bath or a swim it is important that a child is dried down carefully. This includes the genital area and feet. Moist skin between the toes will become soft and then runs the risk of being infected by fungi (athlete's foot/ringworm). This causes itching, the skin becomes further cracked with scratching and the infection is perpetuated. Vaginal infection in small girls is often due to improper cleaning and drying of the vaginal area. It is important that children have their own towels and toothbrushes, if they share them they are more likely to pass on infections to each other.

A very common example of poor hygiene is infection with lice (see page 55). An example of poor education in **hygiene is the** habit which some children acquire of eating dirt. This is called pica (see page 75). Some children will eat just about everything unless they are actively discouraged from doing so. This is more common in deprived children, who then run the risk of lead poisoning.

Instruction should also be given to children about maintaining hygiene whenever they are away from home. Little girls should be told to put paper on strange toilet seats (to avoid contact-acquired disease), even at school and little boys discouraged from leaning against urinals. Make sure that hand washing becomes a habit wherever they are.

## Dental hygiene
See pages 141–2.

## Pets
Only in rare cases does a pet present a health hazard to your child. All pets should, however, be properly looked at by a vet at least once every one to two years both for your sake and theirs, during which time they can have any necessary vaccinations and be treated to clear any worms. Dogs and cats carry diseases such as scabies, fleas, salmonella, ringworm, cat scratch fever and toxacara. Even budgerigars can be dangerous; they can carry an illness known as psitticosis which affects the lungs. Animal fur can cause allergies such as asthma and animal bites can lead to tetanus. All these problems, except possibly fleas, are rare. Most pets are harmless and healthy but care needs to be taken that they stay that way.

## Bottle sterilization
With formula feeding both plastic and glass bottles are used. It is important that these are kept clean as milk is a good medium for bacteria to grow in. There are two sterilizing methods in use. Firstly, with glass bottles, they can be sterilized by boiling for at least 5 minutes. The second method is a chemical method which is the only practical method when plastic bottles are used and is the common practice for glass ones as it is less trouble. The bottles and teats should be cleaned first in ordinary clean

washing-up water and then placed in a commercial sterilizing solution for two to three hours. When the bottle is taken out, allow it to drip dry. Remember, too, that when bottles full of milk are allowed to stand for any length of time, particularly if warm, they are a good medium for bacterial growth to develop. If you are making up feeds in advance, store the bottles in a refrigerator and always throw away any milk left over in the bottle at the end of a feed.

# Prevention of common problems

The key to the prevention of common problems, both physical and emotional is anticipation.

## A new arrival

This is a common occurrence in most families but can be distressing for existing children, particularly if major changes are necessary. To limit the upset of a new arrival, even the youngest child should be informed of what is going to happen. He should be allowed to feel the mother's abdomen and be told what is going on. Attempts should be made to make him feel more secure. If it is necessary for children to begin sharing rooms then this should be done so that they are settled in well before the new child is born.

## Preparation for school

This is a very important event in a child's life. It brings with it a total change of routine. Careful preparation of the child before school will help limit potential problems, such as refusing to go to school and bad behaviour once at school. It is a good idea to make a few pre-school visits so that teachers, rooms and furniture are familiar by the time term starts. Attendance at kindergarten often helps.

## Emotional illness

Psychiatric illness is rare in children. Behavioural problems such as aggressiveness and shyness are, however, common (see also pages 24–5). Problems are greater when children come from unhappy homes and broken families. It is important that a child be offered a comforting and secure environment. Health visitors and social workers are specifically trained to help families undergoing stress and will be able to offer help on housing, finance and the provision of school meals, etc.

## Infectious disease

If one of your children has an infectious disease, make sure that he is isolated until he is out of the infectious period (see pages 125–7). Find out, too, how the disease is passed on so that you can take steps to prevent transfer. If the disease cannot find a way of being carried from one host to another then it will eventually be eradicated. A classic example of this is malaria, which is carried by mosquitoes. If you destroy the mosquitoes, you also destroy the malaria bugs.

Nearer to home, great care is taken that our water supply does not become contaminated, as this is a potentially easy way for a disease to be carried and infect large numbers of people.

## Family crises

Don't forget your child is not immune from the effects of family turmoil. What affects you, even a business worry, may in some way affect the child. Children react in funny ways to parents' distress; some become more naughty, others shy and withdrawn. It will help if they understand that your irritability or short temper is not directed primarily at them. You may even unknowingly neglect your child, but try not to. If he is old enough, explain the problem, apologize if necessary, if he is too young to understand, don't believe he will be unaffected. Be open and honest, go for a walk together, the danger is that a vicious cycle of crisis, parent upset, child upset, parent angry, child sad and so on, can be set up. This clearly should be avoided.

Sometimes the crisis is expected, such as a prearranged hospital stay for you or a close relative. It is best to give your child a reasonable forewarning of this to give him time to get used to the idea.

You cannot keep a death in the family from your child, and a proper explanation is often better than feeding a fantasy. Most children accept death as real if it is explained simply and they need to be allowed to grieve like anybody else. They may react to your reactions or temporarily become more difficult. Time is the usual healer.

## Change

Any unexpected change of routine can be stressful for a child. Moving house and leaving friends, starting a new school can all provoke fears and anxieties. If your child is worried, talk about the change in terms of an adventure and stress the fact that the basic family is still there. First time experiences, such as having a babysitter, or staying away from home or the first visit to the dentist can also upset your child. Explain what will happen before it happens, reassure him and be patient with his fears, so that you limit the problems both for him and you. Change and insecurity often go hand-in-hand in the child, confidence and excitement only come later.

## Accidents

See previous information, pages 159–166.

# PART FOUR
# FIRST AID

# First Aid

Every home should have a first aid kit and every car should carry one. It can be quite simple. It should include such things as tapes and dressings, antiseptics, thermometer, safety pins, scissors and bandages.

It is necessary to call the doctor or go to the nearest hospital casualty department, in the following cases:

(a) Any bleeding which will not stop by simple measures.

(b) Evidence of internal bleeding such as that caused by a significant accident. The child will look pale, be in pain, possibly severely bruised, confused and look generally ghastly.

(c) Bleeding from the nose or ear after a blow to the head. This may imply a fracture at the base of the skull.

(d) A deep wound with debris or a foreign body embedded in it.

(e) A deep puncture wound (as caused by a knife or nail).

(f) An animal bite.

(g) A significant electric shock.

(h) Choking on a foreign body (e.g. an inhaled nut).

(i) A significant burn or scald.

(j) Any loss of consciousness.

(k) Any suggestion of poisoning.

## Mouth-to-mouth respiration and resuscitation

Parents should learn how to carry out artificial respiration and resuscitation. Mouth-to-mouth respiration (kiss of life) can be used in any situation where breathing has stopped. To do this, lay the child on his back, turn his head to one side and clear any debris from the mouth. Tilt the head back and expel only the amount of air that is in your cheeks, when they are blown out, into the child's mouth, whilst pinching his nose. In older children you do use some of the air in your chest. The chest should be seen to move upwards with each breath if you are doing it properly. External cardiac (heart) massage can also be carried out if no heart beat can be felt. You should be very much more gentle with a child than you would be with an adult; the pressure of two to three fingers is usually enough. The pressure is applied rhythmically over the area of the sternum (breast bone).

One needs to give one breath to every three to four pulses of cardiac massage. You *can* give cardiac massage at the same time as mouth-to-mouth resuscitation.

mild disinfectant

cotton bandages

Antiseptic Cream

antiseptic cream

box of plasters (various sizes)

plasters

packet of sterilized gauze dressings for cuts

STERILE 5 GAUZE PADS

crêpe bandages

large triangular bandages to make slings or folded to bind dressing on to wound

adhesive tape

STERILIZED COTTON WOOL

safety pins

sterilized cotton wool for cleaning wounds or for padding around wounds

blunt ended scissors

tweezers

thermometer

*Every home and car should have a functional first aid kit. It need not be elaborate; you need only antiseptic, bandages and simple dressings as shown here. Scissors, tweezers, etc, are useful additions.*

# Mouth-to-mouth resuscitation

*Everyone should learn how to carry out mouth-to-mouth resuscitation for use in emergencies, when an adult or child has stopped breathing. The principle is the same for a child as for an older person, the only difference being in the amount of air you blow into the chest (see below).*

With the head to one side, quickly make sure that the mouth is clear of saliva and any debris, then bring the tongue forward.

Next tilt the head back with one hand on the forehead and the other raising the chin. This straightens out the wind pipe.

Still holding the chin with one hand, pinch the nose with the other, so the air you breathe in does not escape this way.

In a young child, use only the air in your cheeks. Check that you are making the chest move up and down.

Let the air out of the child by itself and then blow in more air through the mouth until the child breathes by himself.

When the child is breathing again, turn him so that he is lying with his head to one side (the recovery position).

# Cardiac massage

*If no heart beat is felt (either in the chest or at the wrist, neck or groin by taking the pulse) and the child is blue, external massage of the heart is necessary to keep the circulation going. Use this in combination with mouth-to-mouth resuscitation. Start by giving a blow to the chest, then give massage.*

*With a small baby, use only the pressure of two fingers and press down 4 to 5 times for every breath you give.*

*In the toddler, you can apply slightly more pressure by using three to four fingers with the same frequency.*

*In the older child, you should again increase the amount of pressure by using your whole hand.*

*In the adolescent, you may need to use two hands, one on top of the other to achieve the right amount of pressure.*

# The recovery position

*Once the child appears to be breathing again, check that the circulation is restored by taking the pulse at the wrist, neck or groin. The child's appearance should have become pink again; no longer blue. Then place him in the recovery position as illustrated and call an ambulance.*

# Common problems

**(1) Nose bleed.** Using two fingers, pinch the nostrils together at the point of the nose where it is soft just below the bone. Keep up the pressure for about ten minutes. The bleeding will usually stop. If the bleeding is excessive and refuses to stop it may be necessary to have the nose properly packed with gauze by a doctor or in hospital (see also page 71).

*Tilt the head backwards or forwards (not much difference which; with forward tilt it is less likely the child will swallow blood, which may make him vomit later).*

**(2) Wounds and grazes.** Wounds should be cleaned with either an antiseptic or salt-to-taste water (see page 122) to remove debris. Afterwards a dry gauze dressing is usually all that is necessary. Very occasionally if the wound was caused by a rusty object or happened in the garden a tetanus injection is needed. If the wound is gaping then stitches may be required so that healing can take properly without an ugly scar forming. Open wounds on the face should be stitched if only for cosmetic reasons. Bleeding is usually controlled by a firm bandage.

*Clean the wound with light antiseptic or water, wiping along the cut, before applying a dry dressing.*

**(3) Swallowed object.** Usually something which gets in will get out at the other end. The stool should be checked until the item has been passed. If there is any doubt, call the doctor. He may advise an X-ray.

**(4) Choking on a foreign body.** This is always frightening. You can try putting the child over your knee and slapping his back between the shoulder blades or try holding him upside down. The best method, however, is a gentle rapid squeeze below the chest which attempts to dislodge the object and allow the child to cough it out. This works by suddenly increasing the pressure inside the chest cage to squeeze the object out. When a child cannot breath, you may need to actively resuscitate him (see pages 176–7).

*When a young child is choking, put him over your knee and gently thump his back to dislodge the object.*

These are all obviously emergency measures. The doctor may need to remove the object, such as a fish or chicken bone, under direct vision in an operating theatre. It is probably best not to reach back into the throat and pick at the object as this may cause vomiting and cause the child to inhale his vomit. This can have quite serious consequences. Remember peanuts are often inhaled; the child throws the nut up, tries to catch it in his mouth, it goes down the wrong way into his lungs – he chokes! Inhaled nuts can cause major problems. If there is any suggestion of an inhaled foreign body, a chest X-ray is necessary.

*For an older child, stand behind and give a gentle, rapid squeeze below the rib cage.*

**(5) Foreign body in the eye.**
Try to discourage the child
from rubbing his eye. If the eye
is bleeding, do nothing
but call your doctor.
Otherwise wash the eye in cold
or lukewarm tap water or water
which has had a little salt added
to it. The aim is to wash out the
object. If this does not work or if
the foreign object is thought
to be a splinter (particularly
if metal) see your doctor.

**(6) Other sites for foreign bodies.** It is not uncommon for
children to put foreign bodies, such as peas, etc., in their nose or
in their ear. Insects occasionally will crawl into a child's ear.
Never probe either the nose or the ear. To get an object out of
the nose try to induce sneezing, for example, with pepper. For
the ear, particularly if you suspect an insect is inside, put in a
few drops of olive oil or mineral oil. This will usually suffocate
the insect. It can then be syringed out by a doctor or nurse.

**(7) Electric shock.** You must
break the contact between the
child and the electricity, for
example, by pulling out
the plug, but be careful.
If you cannot get to the
plug, use something non-
conductive, such as plastic or
wood (a broom handle is ideal)
to drag the child away from
the source of the electricity.
If you touch the child directly
without switching off the
current, you will be electrocuted
as well. In severe cases you
may need to resuscitate your
child (see page 176–7).

**(8) Convulsions.** It is important not to restrain a child who is having a convulsion, or to pour cold water on him in an attempt to rouse him. Lie him down and turn his head sideways and downwards so he does not choke on any vomit. Don't give him any food or drink or put a spoon between his teeth. He can be sponged down (see page 120) if the convulsion is related to a high temperature. He should be left lying face down until a doctor's advice is obtained.

**(9) Fractures.** Fractures with open wounds should not be straightened out by untrained people. Any bleeding should be stopped by gentle pressure over the wound. Continued spurting arterial bleeding may require you to apply a tourniquet to the limb. Just about anything can be used as a tourniquet: belt, tie or stocking will do. Tie this firmly around the limb above the bleeding site and tighten it till the bleeding stops or slows. The tourniquet must be gently released every ten minutes or so, so that the tissues below continue to get blood periodically. Lie the child down for comfort. If the bleeding is not severe, cover the wound with a clean dressing. Then phone for an ambulance or take the child to a hospital casualty department yourself. To immobilize the fracture prior to transport tie the two legs together in several places (if the leg is broken) or bind the arm (if an arm is affected) to the body.

*Before moving a child with a broken leg, tie both limbs to a splint in at least two places.*

*A broken arm should be placed in a sling, as shown, and then this should be secured to the chest with another tie.*

**(10) Splinters.** If you can see the splinter protruding it may be possible to remove it with tweezers. Alternatively, use a needle which has first been sterilized in a flame and then allowed to cool in order to prize out the splinter.

**(11) Loss of consciousness/concussion.** Should a patient be knocked unconscious by a blow or a fall, there may be the added complication of a skull fracture or alternatively some internal brain bleeding. Care must be taken to keep the child's airway free. To do this, lie the child with his face sideways and down to keep his tongue forward and prevent inhalation of any vomit. Call a doctor straightaway. With mild concussion your child may appear to be dazed and confused. Again, seek advice, so that you can be sure there is no fracture or internal injury.

**(12) Drowning.** It is important that young children are supervised when they are near water; pools, ponds and streams, and even bathtubs are potential hazards. When the child sinks, water floods into the lungs and dilutes the circulation. If you find a child in the water, get him out quickly, briefly hold his head down to let any water in the mouth and throat run out, give mouth-to-mouth resuscitation and cardiac massage, if necessary, (see pages 176–7) and call an ambulance immediately. Even near-drowning can cause major problems, so the child will be kept in hospital for observation.

**(13) Burns.** There are three main types of burns:
(a) caustic burns caused by chemicals such as strong acids, alkalis, etc.
(b) scalds caused by over-hot liquids or fats such as from the stove and
(c) dry burns caused by fire, hot materials, electricity or the sun.
The seriousness of the burn depends on the area of skin involved and the depth to which the burn has gone. The terms first, second and third degree burns refer to the depth of the burn and the amount of skin thickness involved; if the full layer of skin is involved it is called a third degree burn. The presence or absence of pain is not a good guide to the burn's seriousness. With deep burns nerve endings can be destroyed, so that no pain is felt.
The simple treatment of most burns is to apply cold water to

the affected area; with chemical burns you should wash the area affected with plenty of water. With extensive burns your child may be in a state of shock and resuscitation will be necessary. The child will look pale and distressed and you may have difficulty rousing him. With severe burns call an ambulance immediately. Do not apply anything but dry dressings to burns until you have seen your doctor. With simple small burns and scalds, after washing a soothing ointment covered by a dry dressing can be used. Mild analgesics, such as paracetamol or aspirin, can be used for the pain.

Children playing near open fires occasionally catch fire or their clothes do; the first thing to do is put out the fire. Roll the child over and over. If you have a blanket or carpet handy do it in that. When the fire is out, cover the child in a wet sheet and arrange for an ambulance. When old enough to understand children should be taught this technique to use on themselves if necessary. Smoke detectors in the home are worth every penny so as to warn the family of fire or smoke; both can kill or injure.

*Minor Burns*

*Major fire burn*

*The best emergency treatment for a minor burn is to rinse it in lots of cold water. Afterwards, use only dry dressings.*

*Flames must be put out immediately. Roll the child in a carpet or blanket to smother the fire. Then cover him with a wet sheet and make him comfortable.*

# Poisoning

A child can be poisoned by many things. Even a mild overdose of common drugs such as sedatives, tranquillizers, aspirin, paracetamol, iron tablets or vitamin tablets can seriously poison a child. Common household items such as perfumes, alcohol, nail varnish, paints, petrol, etc., can also be dangerous. Several types of plant if eaten, including such standbys as the daffodil, can cause abdominal upsets. The child should be discouraged from eating mushrooms and wild berries as these can also occasionally cause poisoning.

There are, however, many items which children swallow but which are in fact not dangerous. These include caps from toy pistols, crayons, felt tip pens, and pencils. Occasionally the child will chew the end of a thermometer, the mercury in that form is not harmful. If a child has taken a drug, or swallowed bulbs, seeds or wild berries, and then feels unwell, call your doctor. The possible indications that your child has been poisoned are vomiting and diarrhoea, pain, convulsions, rapid breathing, and loss of consciousness. When a child is taken to a hospital or doctor, any empty bottles, labels, pills or plants should be taken with him for identification, so that specific treatment can be given. Ipecac syrup should be kept at home; this is a gentle remedy to cause vomiting. If the child has just taken tablets and is wide awake then it is safe to induce vomiting. You should never induce vomiting if the child appears drowsy or if the ingested substance is known to be caustic. Most poisoning is preventable by taking sensible precautions at home (see pages 161–2). If you are in doubt, call your doctor or go straight to the nearest hospital casualty department.

# SPECIAL ORGANIZATIONS

**National Society for the Prevention of Cruelty to Children**
1 Riding House Street, London W1P 8AA
01-580 8812

**Association for all Speech Impaired Children**
347 Central Market, London EC1A 9NH
01-236 3632   01-236 6487

**Asthma Research Council**
12–14 Pembridge Square, London W2 4EH
01-229 1149

**National Association for Gifted Children**
1 South Audley Street, London W1Y 6JS
01-499 1188

**National Society for Autistic Children**
1a Golders Green Road, London NW11 8EA
01-458 4375

**National Society for Mentally Handicapped Children**
117–123 Golden Lane, London EC1
01-253 9433

**Royal National Institute for the Blind**
224 Great Portland Street, London W1N 6AA
01-388 1266

**Royal National Institute for the Deaf**
105 Gower Street, London WC1E 6AH
01-387 8033

**Spastics Society**
12 Park Crescent, London W1N 4EQ
01-636 5020

**British Diabetic Association**
10 Queen Anne Street, London W1M 0BD
01-323 1531

**British Epilepsy Association**
Crowthorne House, New Wokingham Road, Wokingham,
Berks RG11 3AY

**National Cycling Proficiency Scheme Royal Society for the
Prevention of Accidents**
Cannon House, Priory Queensway
Birmingham B4 6BS

# INDEX